THE SARASVATĪ FLOWS ON

THE SARASVATĪ FLOWS ON

The Continuity of Indian Culture

BY

B.B. LAL

Aryan Books International

New Delhi

The Sarasvatī Flows On

ISBN-978-81-7305-202-6

First Published: 2002

Reprinted in 2016 by

Aryan Books International

Pooja Apartments, 4B, Ansari Road, New Delhi-110 002 (India)

Tel.: 23287589, 23255799; Fax: 91-11-23270385

E-mail: aryanbooks@gmail.com

www.aryanbooks.co.in

Designed and Printed in India by

ABI Prints & Publishing Co., New Delhi

To
my revered mother,
Late Shrimati Sarayu Devi,
and others like her
through whom has been flowing
the eternal stream of Indian culture
—tradition, compassion and spirituality—
is this little book dedicated

CONTENTS

Preface ix
Acknowledgements xi
List of Illustrations xiii

I. The Sarasvatī in the *Ṛigveda* **1**
(i) The Sarasvatī as a River 1
(ii) The Sarasvatī as a River-Deity 4
(iii) The Sarasvatī elevated as a goddess 5
(iv) The Sarasvatī as an Āprī Deity 5
(v) The Sarasvatī as *Vāk* 5

II. The Sarasvatī on the Terra Firma **7**
(i) Some Erroneous Views 7
(ii) The Correct Identification, based on a Correlation between the Ṛigvedic Geography and Ground Realities 11
(iii) The Source and Perennial Water-supply 16
(iv) When and How did the Sarasvatī Dry up? 22

III. The Most Ancient Civilization of the Sarasvatī Valley **25**
(i) Introductory 25
(ii) Its Adolescence 26
(iii) At Maturity 45
(iv) The Myths of 'Aryan Invasion' and 'Extinction' of the Harappan Civilization 67

(v) The Late Harappan Scenario in the Sarasvatī Valley and Beyond 77

IV. The Cultural Stream Flows on 82

(i) Ornaments, Make-up and Toiletry 82

(ii) Games and Recreation 89

(iii) House- and town-planning 93

(iv) Cooking and Associated Items 95

(v) Agriculture and Water-management 98

(vi) Transport, on Land and Water 107

(vii) Crafts 110

(viii) And Folk Tales too 114

(ix) Religion 116

(x) Social Hierarchy 129

(xi) The Script: Its Continuance — A Matter of Debate 132

V. In Retrospect 136

Bibliography 137

Index 141

PREFACE

Two different reasons have impelled me to write this little book. One is the persistent assertion by Western linguists and historians and their, more vociferous, Indian counterparts that the Ṛigvedic Sarasvatī was the Helmand of Afghanistan. As would be shown in this book, this assumption is completely baseless. The Ṛigvedic Sarasvatī, according to what is stated in the *Ṛigveda* itself (*RV* 10. 75. 5) lay between the Yamunā on the one hand and the Sutlej on the other. These two rivers do not exist in Afghanistan. Thus, how can the Ṛigvedic Sarasvatī be located there? Again, the *Ṛigveda* (*RV* 3. 23. 4) refers to the Dṛiṣadvatī and Āpayā as being the tributaries of the Sarasvatī. These two rivers are in Haryana (India) and not in Afghanistan. Further, according to the Vedic evidence (*RV* 7. 95. 2), the Sarasvatī rose in the mountains and fell into the sea. There is no sea in Afghanistan and the Helmand never ever joined the sea. It is thus absolutely clear that the Helmand cannot be the Ṛigvedic Sarasvatī. As the following pages would show, the Ṛigvedic Sarasvatī is none other than the river which in its upper reaches is still known as the Sarasvatī in Haryana, joins the Ghaggar and after a while dries up near Sirsa. Thereafter it goes by the names of the Ghaggar in Rajasthan, Hakra in Cholistan (Pakistan) and Nara in Sindh. Finally, it fell into the Rann of Kachchh, way east of the present-day Indus.

The second reason is a desire to share with others the knowledge that the most ancient civilization of the Indian subcontinent, known variously as the Harappan, Indus or Indus-Sarasvati Civilization, was not destroyed (much less by Aryan invaders, as propounded by one school of thought). Whether this civilization was the creation of the Aryans themselves is a matter which cannot be established as long as the Harappan script remains undeciphered. (Unfortunately, none of the dozen or more claimants has really hit the mark.) Be that as it may, a hard fact that stands out is that even today there is no walk of life in which we cannot discern the grass-root features of this ancient civilization: be it agriculture, cooking habits, arts, crafts, games, ornaments, toiletry, religious practices or social stratification. If you wish to be greeted with *namaste*, a Harappan terracotta would be only too glad to do so (Fig. 4. 66). Or if you wanted to join a class in *yoga*, the Mohenjo-darians would welcome you (Fig. 4. 67). A Kalibanganite of 2800 BC would be ready to accept your 'order' for *tandūrī rotī*s (Fig. 4. 25). If you are a farmer from Haryana or Rajasthan, you should not get crossed with your five-thousand-year-old Sarasvatī valley counterpart in case he insisted that you have borrowed the criss-cross pattern of ploughing the field from him (Figs. 4. 31-34). Above all, you should not be taken aback if you find that the practice of applying *sindūra* (vermilion) to the *sīmanta/māṅga* (line of partition of the hair on the head) by Hindu womenfolk is rooted back in the Harappan Civilization itself (Figs. 4. 1a & b). The culture that once flowered on the banks of the Sarasvatī still flows on. Isn't it wonderful ?

New Delhi **B. B. Lal**

May 20, 2000

ACKNOWLEDGEMENTS

There is a very senior colleague of mine whom I have always admired and, I am sure, will continue to do so for the rest of my life. This is Shri Krishna Deva, who even at the age of 85 is as alert, active and productive as ever. But this is not the only reason why I admire him. He has something which I do not have: this is absolute composure in the midst of calamities under which any normal human being would break down. He was operated upon for prostate cancer a couple of years ago. He was again hospitalized for a serious illness a few months back. But whenever I called on him he invariably enquired of me about the progress of this book which, he knew, I was busy with. And then came the unbelievable climax. His wife passed away in the first half of May and when my wife and I went to his house to offer our condolences, we met a completely composed Krishna Deva; and, to cap it all, amidst other things that we talked about was once again his enquiry about the book. Since the first draft was ready, after a few days I handed it over to him for perusal. He has not just gone through it but has made many valuable suggestions. I really do not know in what manner I should offer my deeply felt gratitude to him. Perhaps no words can do that. I can only pray to the Lord to give him long and healthy life, so that he can continue to inspire me.

As mentioned in the Preface, many cultural traits of the Harappan Civilization continue even to this day. This feature formed a part of the First Foundation Day Lecture at the Delhi Institute of Heritage Research and Management, delivered by me on the 23rd of April, 2000. The Director of the Institute, Professor Dr. Makkhan Lal, helped me a great deal in preparing several slides of modern subjects, which I used in the lecture and am using for this book as well. Shri Ashwini Asthana of his office also helped me in this regard. To both of them I am most grateful.

I have also borrowed some illustrations from Dr. Jonathan Mark Kenoyer's book, *Ancient Cities of the Indus Civilization,* and am thus under personal obligation to him. Likewise, I am indebted to Dr. J.-F. Jarrige for certain illustrations. Shri R.S. Bisht and Dr. Amarendra Nath have been kind enough to lend me some of their unpublished photographs which provide clear evidence of the use of spoked wheels during the Harappan time. To both of them I am deeply beholden. Further, I would like to record my gratefulness to Drs. V.M.K. Puri, B.C. Verma, Yash Pal and his collegues, M.R. Mughal and Louis Flam from whose publications I have used certain maps.

There are at least four other persons whom I would like to thank. They are: Dr. R.D. Choudhury and Shri D.P. Sharma, for help in preparing photographs of some objects in the National Museum, New Delhi; Shri S.K. Sharma, for recasting the maps appearing in this book; and Shri Vishnu Kant, for help in proof-reading and indexing.

It would be a formality to thank my wife, Kusum, for all the help she has been giving me from time to time. In fact, she resents my mentioning her name, but I am sorry I cannot help doing so.

Finally, it is my publisher, Shri Vikas Arya, for whom I have always had a word of praise. Any publisher would like to make money out of his business, but there are some good points about Vikas: he is receptive and is keen on making a good job of his publications.

LIST OF ILLUSTRATIONS

2.1 Synoptic view of the lower Indus valley, showing the possible course of the Sarasvatī beyond Marot through the Nara into the Rann of Kachchha. The Rann is conspicuous because of the high reflectance (white tone) of its encrustation. (Landsat imagery, after Yash Pal *et al.* 1984)

2.2 Lower Sindh and Kachchh in the 3rd millennium BC. (After Louis Flam 1999)

2.3 Origin of the Vedic Sarasvatī from the Himalayas. (After V.M.K. Puri and B.C. Verma 1998)

2.4 Drainage Pattern of the Vedic Sarasvatī in the Himalayas. (After V.M.K. Puri and B.C. Verma 1998)

2.5 The Sarasvatī Basin in the 3rd Millennium BC

2.6. Areas of Hakra Ware and Early, Mature and Late Harappan Sites. (After M.R. Mughal 1992)

2.7 Appearance of Bata-Markanda Divide. (After V.M.K. Puri and B.C. Verma 1998)

3.1 Kunal: Pottery, painted with two colours: black outline and white in-filling. Early Harappan. (Courtesy J.S. Khatri and M. Acharya)

3.2 Kunal: Silver ornaments. Early Harappan. (Courtesy J.S. Khatri and M. Acharya)

3.3 Kalibangan: Early Harappan settlement.

3.4 Kalibangan: Lane with adjacent houses. Early Harappan. (Courtesy Archaeological Survey of India)

3.5 Kalibangan: Early Harappan structures. (Courtesy ASI)

3.6 Kalibangan: Early Harappan pottery. Solid line or filling denotes black colour; hatching, white.

3.7 Kalibangan: Faulted strata, resulting from an earthquake which brought about the end of the Early Harappan settlement. (Courtesy ASI)

3.8 Kalibangan: Faulted walls of the Early Harappan Period, resulting from an earthquake. (Courtesy ASI)

3.9 Rakhigarhi: General plan of the site. (Courtesy Amarendra Nath)

3.10 Kalibangan: Harappan settlement, Period II.

3.11 Kalibangan: Brick-on-edge pathway, running along the northern side of the partition-wall of the Citadel. Mature Harappan. (Courtesy ASI)

3.12 Kalibangan: The widest (7.2 m) street in the Lower Town. Mature Harappan. (Courtesy ASI)

3.13 Kalibangan: Another street in the Lower Town. Mature Harappan. (Courtesy ASI)

3.14 A drain discharging into a soakage jar embedded in the street immediately outside the house. Mature Harappan. (Courtesy ASI)

3.15 Kalibangan: Terracotta bull. Mature Harappan.

3.16 Kalibangan: Bronze bull. Mature Harappan.

3.17 Kalibangan: Cylinder seal and its impression. Mature Harappan.

3.18 Kalibangan: Terracotta *kernos*. Mature Harappan.

3.19 Kalibangan: Grave 29. Mature Harappan.

3.20 Kalibangan: Burial in a circular pit, with pottery, bronze mirror, etc., but without skeletal remains. Mature Harappan.

3.21 Banawali Excavations. (After R.S. Bisht 1994)

3.22 Banawali: Section across the moat. Mature Harappan. (Courtesy ASI)

3.23 Banawali: An apsidal structure associated with 'fire-altars'. Mature Harappan. (Courtesy ASI)

3.24 Rakhigarhi: A pottery-kiln. Mature Harappan. (Courtesy ASI)

3.25 Rakhigarhi: Burial; mark the shell bangles on the left wrist. Mature Harappan. (Courtesy ASI)

3.26 Surkotada: Horse bones. Mature Harappan. (Courtesy ASI)

3.27 Lothal: Terracotta horse. Mature Harappan. (Courtesy ASI)

3.28 Rakhigarhi: Terracotta wheel. The painted lines radiating from the central hub and reaching the circumference clearly represent the spokes of the wheel. Mature Harappan. (Courtesy ASI)

3.29 Kalibangan: Like the Rakhigarhi example, this terracotta wheel too is painted, depicting spokes. Mature Harappan. (Courtesy ASI)

3.30 Banawali: Terracotta wheels showing the spokes in low relief. The specimen on the left is worn out but the spokes may still be seen. The specimen on the right, though broken, shows the spokes very clearly. Mature Harappan. (Courtesy ASI)

3.31 Hastināpura: Terracotta wheel, showing spokes in low relief. Śuṅga-Kushan times. (Courtesy ASI)

3.32 Hulas: Pottery types. Late Harappan. (After K.N. Dikshit 1982)

3.33 Alamgirpur: Late Harappan pottery including a three-legged *chakalā* bearing an inscription on the underside. (After Y.D. Sharma)

4.1a & 4.1b Nausharo: Terracotta female figures, painted. The yellow colour on ornaments suggests that these were made of gold; the hair is black, while the red on the line of partition of the hair indicates the use of vermilion. Period IB, 2800-2600 BC. (Courtesy J.-F. Jarrige and J.M. Kenoyer)

4.2 Bihar Chief Minister Shrimati Rabri Devi and her husband Shri Laloo Prasad Yadava, in the State capital, Patna. Mark the vermilion in the *māṅga* of the lady, which is an indicator of her marital status.

4.3 Mohenjo-daro: Gold cone. Mature Harappan. (Courtesy National Museum, New Delhi)

4.4 A newly married lady, on the right, wearing a conical ornament on the head (covered by the *dupattā*). She also wears bangles all over her right arm. (Courtesy Makkhan Lal)

4.5 Kunal: Discular beads of silver, having perforation along the diameter. Early Harappan. (Courtesy J.S. Khatri and M. Acharya)

4.6 Lothal: Discular beads of gold, having perforation along the diameter. Mature Harappan.

4.7 Mohenjo-daro: The famous bronze figure of a 'dancing girl', wearing spiralled bangles on the upper left arm. Mature Harappan.

4.8 Kunal: Spiralled bangles, silver. Early Harappan. (Courtesy J.S. Khatri and M. Acharya)

4.9 A woman wearing spiralled bangles. (Courtesy Makkhan Lal)

4.10 Mohenjo-daro: Ivory comb with teeth on two opposite sides. Mature Harappan.

4.11 Harappa: A three-in-one toiletry gadget, copper. Mature Harappan. (Courtesy National Museum, New Delhi)

4.12 A modern three-in-one toiletry gadget, copper. (Courtesy Makkhan Lal)

4.13 Children at Harappa, playing with pottery discs the game called *piṭṭu*. (Courtesy J.M. Kenoyer)

4.14 Harappa: Pottery discs from Mature Harappan levels. (Courtesy J.M. Kenoyer)

4.15 Rakhigarhi: A stack of pottery discs, *in situ* in a Mature Harappan stratum. (Courtesy ASI)

4.16 Lothal: Terracotta gamesmen. Mature Harappan. (Courtesy ASI)

4.17 Use of gamesmen in chess; reconstruction by S.R. Rao. The Lothal gamesmen are on the left and the modern ones on the right.

4.18 Mohenjo-daro: Cubical dice in terracotta, with 1-6 blind holes on respective faces. Mature Harappan. (Courtesy National Museum, New Delhi)

4.19 Modern example of cubical dice, with 1-6 blind holes on respective faces. (Courtesy Makkhan Lal)

4.20 Mohenjo-daro: Terracotta dog, wearing a collar. Mature Harappan.

4.21 Harappa: Terracotta cage, with birds. Mature Harappan. (Courtesy National Museum, New Delhi)

4.22 Modern example of keeping birds in a cage. (Courtesy Makkhan Lal)

4.23 Kalibangan: Part of the fortification-wall around the citadel, showing alternate courses of headers and stretchers (now called the English bond). Mature Harappan. (Courtesy ASI)

4.24 Kalibangan: Successive floors of clay with soling of terracotta nodules and charcoal, in a house in Lower Town. Mature Harappan. (Courtesy ASI)

4.25 Kalibangan: Clay *tandūrs* (cooking ovens). Early Harappan. (Courtesy ASI)

4.26 A modern three-legged *pātā,* used for rolling bread. (Courtesy Makkhan Lal)

4.27 Some Mature Harappan metal utensils.

4.28 Kalibangan: Terracotta feeding cup. Mature Harappan.

4.29 Mohenjo-daro: Pottery *kamaṇḍalu*s. Mature Harappan.

4.30 A Sādhū with a *kamaṇḍalu* by his side. (Courtesy Makkhan Lal)

4.31 Kalibangan: An agricultural field, showing criss-cross pattern of the furrows. Early Harappan. (Courtesy ASI)

4.32 Kalibangan: Another view of the same field. (Courtesy ASI)

4.33 Around present Kalibangan village: The system of ploughing the field, which also has the criss-cross pattern of the furrows. (Courtesy ASI)

4.34 Around present Kalibangan village: A field with mustard plants in the widely distanced furrows and those of horse gram in the others. (Courtesy ASI)

4.35 Banawali: Terracotta model of a plough. Mature Harappan. (Courtesy ASI)

4.36 Harappa: Platform of kiln-fired bricks. In the central hollow was fixed a wooden mortar for pounding grains. Mature Harappan. (Courtesy ASI)

4.37 Near Srinagar (Kashmir): Pounding rice with pestles in a wooden mortar. (Courtesy ASI)

4.38 Kalibangan: A well, lined with wedge-shaped bricks, in the courtyard of a house. Mature Harappan.

4.39 Dholavira: A stone-lined well in the Castle. The flat slab of the trough (top left) bears abrasion marks left by the ropes that constantly rubbed against it in the process of drawing water. Mature Harappan. (Courtesy ASI)

4.40 Dholavira: A sketch to illustrate how water was drawn from the well (Fig. 4.39). This very method was in use in northern India prior to the recent introduction of electrically operated tube-wells. (Courtesy Sushama Lal)

4.41 Dholavira: A sketch to illustrate how an adjacent streamlet was dammed and water was brought to a reservoir during the Mature Harappan times. (Courtesy Sushama Lal)

4.42 Kalibangan: Reconstruction of a bullock-cart, on the basis of terracotta samples of frames and wheels. Mature Harappan.

4.43 Harappa: Early cart-tracks beneath Cemetery H. (Courtesy ASI)

4.44 Mohenjo-daro: Impression of a seal, depicting a boat with a cabin. Mature Harappan.

4.45 A modern boat with a cabin, on the Indus in Pakistan. (Courtesy J.M. Kenoyer)

4.46 Lothal: Kiln for bead-making. Mature Harappan. (Courtesy ASI)

4.47. Mohenjo-daro: Belt or necklace of carnelian beads. Mature Harappan. (Courtesy J.M. Kenoyer)

4.48 A stage in the bead-making process, Gujarat. (Courtesy J.M. Kenoyer)

4.49 Kalibangan: Terracotta model of a cot, with the bedspread shown in black-and-white design. Early Harappan. (After Madhu Bala 1997)

4.50 Example of a modern cot, loaded with clothes including printed bedspreads. (Courtesy Makkhan Lal)

4.51 Lothal: A vase, the painting on which appears to narrate the story of 'The Thirsty Crow'. Mature Harappan. (After S.R. Rao 1985)

4.52 Lothal: Painting on another jar seems to narrate the story of 'The Cunning Fox'. Mature Harappan. (After S.R. Rao 1985)

4.53 Mohenjo-daro: Impression of a seal depicting a seated figure surrounded by animals, believed to be Śiva in his aspect of Paśupati (Lord of animals). Mature Harappan. (Courtesy G.L. Possehl)

4.54 Kalibangan: Terracotta *liṅga*-cum-*yoni*. Mature Harappan. (Courtesy ASI)

4.55 Śiva *liṅga* and *yoni* in a modern temple. From the overhead pitcher water-drops keep on dripping on the *liṅga*. (Courtesy Makkhan Lal)

4.56 Harappa: Terracotta tablet, depicting the Śiva-like seated figure (right) and a person attempting to kill a buffalo, perhaps as a sacrifice. Mature Harappan. (Courtesy J.M. Kenoyer)

4.57 Kalibangan: Obverse and reverse of a terracotta 'cake'. On one side is shown a horned deity and on the other an animal pulled by a man with a rope. Mature Harappan. (Courtesy ASI)

4.58 Kalibangan: This brick-lined sacrificial pit, containing bovine bones and antlers, was discovered on a platform in the southern half of the Citadel. Mature Harappan. (Courtesy ASI)

4.59. Kalibangan: A 'fire-altar' in a house in the Lower Town. Mature Harappan. (Courtesy ASI)

4.60 Kalibangan: A row of seven 'fire-altars' discovered on a platform in the southern half of the Citadel. Mature Harappan. (Courtesy ASI)

4.61 Mohenjo-daro: Impression of a seal, showing in the upper register a deity within an enclosure of pipal branches, a kneeling devotee and an animal perhaps brought in for sacrifice. In the lower register there are seven human figures marching in a row. Mature Harappan. (Courtesy G.L. Possehl)

4.62 Mohenjo-daro: The svastika motif engraved on a seal. Mature Harappan.

4.63 Entrance to a Hindu house, painted with svastika symbol on either side. (Courtesy Makkhan Lal)

4.64a Harappa: The head and trunk of a terracotta elephant, painted. Mature Harappan. (Courtesy J.M. Kenoyer)

4.64b Elephants with painted forehead and trunk. (Courtesy J.M. Kenoyer)

4.65 The President of India, Shri K.R. Narayanan (extreme left), being greeted with *namaste* by the Prime Minister, Shri Atal Bihari Vajpayee (extreme right), and other dignitaries on the eve of the President's departure on a foreign tour.

4.66 Harappa: A terracotta figurine greeting with *namaste*. Mature Harappan. (Courtesy G.L. Possehl)

4.67 Terracotta figurines in Yogic *āsana*s: 1-4, from Harappa; 5-6, from Mohenjo-daro. Mature Harappan.

4.68 Mohenjo-daro: Limestone statue of a 'priest'. The introvert eyes are indicative of *dhyāna mudrā* (meditative pose). Mature Harappan. (Courtesy G.L. Possehl)

4.69 Harappa: Citadel and structures under its shadow.

4.70 Mohenjo-daro: Writing tablets (*takhtīs*) represented in terracotta. Mature Harappan. (After E.J.H. Mackay 1938)

4.71 Yamuna Nagar: A third-second century BC terracotta plaque. It shows a child pointing out one of the Brāhmī alphabets written on a *takhtī*. (After Yoganand Shastri)

4.72 School children writing on wooden *takhtīs*. (Courtesy Makkhan Lal)

CHAPTER I

THE SARASVATĪ IN THE *ṚIGVEDA*

The *Ṛigveda* mentions a large number of rivers, from the Gaṅgā in the east to the Indus in the west. However, it is the Sarasvatī alone which has been referred to many a time — maybe nearly fifty. In fact, some of the *Sūktas* have exclusively been devoted to her. She has multiple aspects. First and foremost, she is a river which flows on the terra firma, but may also be visualized as having descended from the heavens. In this latter context she is also regarded as a river-deity. Thirdly, she is just a deity, like any other deity, without any mention of her river-aspect. Fourthly, as a deity she also has an *Āprī* status and is invoked, along with other deities, to be present at sacrifices (*yajña*s). Her yet another aspect is association with the intellect (*dhī*) and perhaps speech (*vāk*), in which capacity she later on takes the form of a full-fledged goddess presiding over learning and fine arts. However, it needs to be added that the Vedic seers were not very much interested in strictly compartmentalizing these different aspects. Hence their occasional overlap. Anyway, we shall deal below, serially, with these various facets of the Sarasvatī.

(I) THE SARASVATĪ AS A RIVER

We begin with the oft-quoted *Nadī-stuti* hymn, viz. 10.75, of which Verses 5 and 6 mention a set of rivers, from the Gaṅgā in the east to the Sindhu (Indus), along with its right-bank tributaries, in the west:

imam me ***Gaṅge Yamune Sarasvati Śutudri*** *stomam sachatā Paruṣṇyā /*
Asiknyā Marudvṛidhe Vitastyā Ārjīkīye śṛiṇuhyā Suṣomayā // 5 //
Tṛiṣṭāmayā prathamam yātave sajūḥ Susartvā Rasayā Śvetyā tyā /
tvam Sindho Kubhayā Gomatīm Krumum Mehatnvā saratham yābhirīyase //6//

O Gaṅgā, Yamunā, Sarasvatī, Śutudrī (Sutlej) and Paruṣṇī (Ravi), O Marudvṛidhā with Asiknī (Chenab), O Ārjikīyā with Vitastā (Jhelum) and Suṣomā (Sohan), please listen to and accept this hymn of mine. [5]*

O Sindhu (Indus), flowing, you first meet the Tṛiṣṭāmā (and then) the Susartu, the Rasā, and the Śvetā (Swat), and thereafter the Kubhā (Kabul), the Gomatī (Gomal), the Krumu (Kurram) with the Mehatnu; and (finally) you move on in the same chariot with them (i.e. carry their waters with you). [6]

It would be seen that altogether nineteen rivers are mentioned in these two verses, although Verse 1 of the same *Sūkta* uses a term *sapta-sapta tredhā* which would seem to mean 'three times seven', i.e. twenty-one. One does not know which two rivers are missing from this list. Perhaps one of these may have been the Vipāś (Beas) which is a tributary of the Sutlej and should have normally been mentioned along with the latter. Anyway, this is not a matter of essence here, since we are primarily concerned in our present enquiry with the Sarasvatī. What is important in this context is that she is mentioned **between** the Yamunā and the Sutlej. The significance of this basic information will be discussed in the next chapter (II) when we take up the identification of the Ṛigvedic Sarasvatī with a present-day river.

Another important information that we get from the *Ṛigveda* is about where the Sarasvatī originated and where it ended. Thus, Verses 7.95.1 and 2 state:

pra kṣodasā dhāyasā sasra eṣā Sarasvatī dharuṇamāyasī pūḥ /
prabābadhānā rathyeva yāti viśvā apo mahinā sindhuranyāḥ // 1 //

ekāchetat Sarasvatī nadīnām śuchir yatī giribhya ā samudrāt */*
rāyaśchetantī bhuvanasya bhūrerghṛitam payo duduhe ***Nāhuṣāya*** *// 2 //*

This Sarasvatī (river) gushes forward with her waters and protects all like a metal fortress; with her might, like a charioteer, she surpasses (lit. obstructs) all other waters (rivers). [1]

Purest amongst all the rivers and vibrant, the **Sarasvatī moves on from the mountains to the ocean**; manifesting immense riches of the world, she has provided milk and *ghee* (clarified butter) to **Nahuṣa**. [2]

From the foregoing verses it is abundantly clear that the **Sarasvatī was a mighty river, originating in the mountains and flowing all the way down to the ocean.**

---

* It is well known that Griffith's translation is faulty at places. I, therefore, give my own translation of the verses quoted here.

The fact that the Sarasvatī was indeed a mighty river is echoed by many other verses in the *Ṛigveda*. See, for example, 6.61.2:

> *iyam śuṣmebhir bisakhā ivārujat sānu girīṇām taviṣebhirūrmibhiḥ /*
> *pārāvataghnīmavase suvṛiktibhiḥ Sarasvatīmā vivāsema dhītibhiḥ //*

> This (Sarasvatī river) has shattered the mountain peaks with her fast and powerful waves, just (as easily) as one uproots the lotus-stems; let us invoke her, who strikes what is far and near, with holy hymns and prayers.

Or, again, 6.61.8:

> *yasyā ananto arhutastveṣaścariṣṇurarṇavaḥ /*
> *amaścharati roruvat //*

> Whose (i.e. of the Sarasvatī) boundless, impetuous and swift-moving flood gushes forth with a tempestuous roar.

While she had ample water of her own, she was also fed by many a tributary, as indicated by the use of such epithets as *saptasvasā* (having seven sisters or being one of the seven sisters). For example, Verse 6.61.10 states:

> *uta naḥ priyā priyāsu saptasvasā sujuṣṭā /*
> *Sarasvatī stomyā bhūt //*

> To us the dearest amongst the dear ones, seven-sistered, (the Sarasvatī) has earned our hymns of praise.

Exactly which these seven sisters were it is difficult to determine. However, the Dṛiṣadvatī and Āpayā seem to have been two of them, as indicated by Verse 3.23.4:

> *ni tvā dadhe vara ā pṛithivyā iḷāyāspade sudinatve ahnām /*
> ***Dṛiṣadvatyām** mānuṣa **Āpayāyām Sarasvatyām** revadagne didīhi //*

> O Agni, I have established you at the best place on the earth, in the dwelling of Iḷā, on this most auspicious of the days; may you shine brilliantly amongst the descendants of Manu, on the banks of the Dṛiṣadvatī, Āpayā and Sarasvatī.

The Dṛiṣadvatī has been identified with the modern Chautang, while Āpayā's identification is somewhat debated. It may have been a river in Kurukṣetra, as indicated by Verse 3.83.68 of the *Mahābhārata*.

In the valley of the Sarasvatī there lived many 'peoples', and many a king ruled there. This is shown by several verses, such as 6.61.12, 7.96.2, 7.95.2 and 8.21.18. Thus, while Verse 6.61.12 —

> *triṣadhasthā saptadhātuḥ* ***Pañch jātā vardhayantī*** */*
> *vāje vāje havyā bhūt //* —

only states that she is the 'promoter of five peoples', without specifying them, Verse 7.96.2 —

> *ubhe yatte mahinā śubhre andhasī adhikṣiyanti* ***Pūravaḥ*** */*
> *sā no bodhyavitrī marutsakhā choda rādho maghonām //* —

specifically mentions the name of the Pūrus.

In so far as the kings who ruled in the Sarasvatī valley, Verse 7.95.2, quoted earlier, mentions the name of **Nahuṣa**. Verse 8.21.18 not only refers to a king called **Chitra** but also indicates that there were other kings of lesser importance —

> ***Chitra id rājā rājakā idanyake yake Sarasvatīm anu*** */*
> *parjanya iva tatanaddhi vṛiṣṭyā sahasramayutā dadat //*

Along the Sarasvatī, Chitra indeed is the king, whereas others are only petty rulers; just as Parjanya gives plenty of rain, so has he (Chitra) given a thousand, nay a myriad, gifts.

(II) THE SARASVATĪ, AS A RIVER-DEITY

Since the Sarasvatī originated in the high mountains and descended therefrom to the plains where dwelt her users, *viz.* the Vedic Aryans, she was regarded by them, in sheer reverence, as a heavenly deity. This is indicated by many verses. Look, for example, at Verse 5.43.11:

> *ā no divo bṛihataḥ parvatādā Sarasvatī yajatā gantu yajñam /*
> *havam devī jujuṣāṇā ghṛitāchī śagmām no vāchamuśatī śṛiṇotu //*

> May the venerable Sarasvatī come to our sacrifice **from the heavens and high mountains**; may she, filled with *ghee* (clarified butter), accept our oblations and listen to our devotional hymns.

Not only has she been regarded as the best of the rivers (*nadītamā*), but has also been acclaimed as **the most respected deity** (***devītamā***). Cf. Verse 2.41.16:

ambitame nadītame devitame Sarasvati /
apraśastā iva smasi praśastimamba naskṛidhi //

O Sarasvati, the best of mothers, the best of rivers, **the best of goddesses**, we are unknown and insignificant, please favour us with renown, O mother.

(III) THE SARASVATĪ, ELEVATED AS A GODDESS

From the concept of a river regarded as a deity, she was elevated to regular deity-hood and was mentioned alongside other deities, such as Agni, Indra, Varuṇa, etc. This is clear, for example, from Verse 5.46.2:

Agna Indra Varuṇa Mitra devāḥ Śardhaḥ pra yanta Mārutota Viṣṇo /
Ubhā Nāsatyā Rudro adha gnāḥ Pūṣā Bhagaḥ ***Sarasvatī*** *juṣanta //*

O gods — Agni, Indra, Varuṇa, Mitra, the Marutas and Viṣṇu, give us strength; O the two Nāsatyas, Rudra, the divine females, Puṣan, Bhaga, **Sarasvatī**, be pleased.

(IV) THE SARASVATĪ AS AN ĀPRĪ DEITY

Then there was yet another kind of transformation in her deity-hood. She was also an Āprī deity, invoked to take her seat at the sacrifices. In this context may well be cited a couple of verses, for example, 1.13.9 and 1.142.9.

Iḷā ***Sarasvatī*** *Mahī tisro devīrmayobhuvaḥ /*
barhiḥ Sīdantvastridhaḥ *//*

May the three goddesses, Ilā, **Sarasvatī** and Mahī, who bring delight and never fail, **be seated on the sacrificial grass**.

Śuchirdeveṣvarpitā hotrā Marutsu Bhāratī /
Ilā ***Sarasvatī*** *Mahī* ***barhiḥ Sīdantu yajñiyāḥ*** *//*

Pure and revered amidst the gods and the Maruts, may Bhāratī, Ilā, **Sarasvatī** and Mahī be **seated on the sacrificial grass**.

(V) THE SARASVATĪ AS *VĀK*

Whether the latter-day concept of the Sarasvatī being a goddess of learning had begun to emerge in the Ṛigvedic times remains unclear. However, her association with *dhī* (intellect) is hinted at in Verse 2.3.8, although herein she still plays the role of an Āprī goddess.

> ***Sarasvatī*** *sādhayantī* ***dhiyam*** *na Iḷā devī Bhāratī viśvatūrtiḥ /*
> *tisro devīḥ svadhayā barhiredamachchhidram pāntu śaraṇam niṣadya //*

> **Sarasvatī**, who prompts our **intellect** (towards higher thoughts), divine Ilā, and Bhāratī who is all-surpassing, may all the three goddesses, on their own volition, sit on the sacrificial grass and protect (the sacrifice).

In Verse 1.3.12 she is said to 'reign over thoughts':

> *maho arṇaḥ* ***Sarasvatī*** *pra chetayati ketunā /*
> ***dhiyo viśvā vi rājati*** *//*

> **Sarasvatī**, with her knowledge, makes one understand this (worldly) ocean and **illumines all intellects**.

CHAPTER II

THE SARASVATĪ ON THE TERRA FIRMA

The colour of the glasses one wears colours the vision one sees. Thus, it is but natural for anyone with a preconceived notion to look at things from that given mindset. And this is precisely what has happened in the case of the identification of the Ṛigvedic Sarasvatī on the terra firma. It would, therefore, be worth while to take note of the glasses looking through which the identification has been made.

(I) SOME ERRONEOUS VIEWS

Way back, in 1786, when Sir William Jones declared at a meeting of the Royal Asiatic Society of Bengal that there was so much in common in the Sanskrit, Greek and Latin languages that these may have had a common origin (Jones 1788), little did he realize that he was inadvertently sowing the seeds of a major controversy. The similarity of these languages led to the formulation of the concept of a race, designated as the Indo-European race, which spoke the mother language lying at the root of the above-mentioned three languages. Soon the competition started for locating the 'original home' of this 'race'. Some said it was in Central Asia, others in Russia, and yet others in northern Europe. It was further argued that from that given region the speakers of the 'mother language' branched off, westward to most of Europe and eastward to India via Iran.

It is against this preconceived notion that the Ṛigvedic culture has been interpreted by most Western scholars and many of their Indian followers. Thus, holding on to the notion of a west-to-east movement, these scholars believe that if there is anything common between the *Āvestā*, which is an ancient Iranian text, and the *Ṛigveda*, which lay further east in India, it is the Avestan evidence that must take precedence over the Ṛigvedic.

Toeing the line of his Western ideologues and being incensed by certain statements of the well known archaeologist S. P. Gupta, R. S. Sharma, a noted Indian historian who was in limelight in the middle 1990s as a Babri Masjid protagonist, blurts out (Sharma 1999: 35):

> The **fundamentalists** want to establish the superiority of the Sarasvatī over the Indus because of **communal** considerations. In the Harappan context they think that after partition the Indus belongs to the Muslims and only the Sarasvatī remains with the Hindus.

He goes on to say (ibid.):

> The Sarasvatī receives much attention in the *Ṛg Veda* and several *sūkta*s are devoted to it; so they want to use it for their purpose. But it seems that there are several Sarasvatis, and the earliest Sarasvatī cannot be identified with the Hakra and the Ghaggar. In the *Ṛg Veda* the Sarasvatī is called the best of the rivers (*nadītama*). It seems to have been a great river with perennial water. The Hakra and the Ghaggar cannot match it. **The earliest Sarasvatī is considered identical with the Helmand in Afghanistan which is called Harakhwati in the *Āvestā*.**

But in the same breath he confesses (ibid.: 35-36):

> But the archaeology of the Helmand valley in the second millennium BC needs adequate attention. Its two large cities Shahr-ī-Sokkta and Mundigak show decay in this period. In place of wheel-turned pottery Mundigak V shows hand-turned pottery. The users of this pottery may have come from outside, but we need more information about them.

In spite of his own confession, he still goes on:

> **In any case the linguistic and time-place proximity of the *Āvestā* to the *Ṛg Veda* leaves no doubt that the early Vedic Sarasvatī is the same as the Harakhwati or the Helmand. As the Vedic people expanded they took the name Sarasvatī to Punjab, Haryana and Rajasthan, and also to Garhwal, Prayaga and Rajgir.**

My earnest request to the R.S. Sharma-clan is to calm down and assess the evidence with an open mind. The necessary evidence is set forth hereunder.

To begin with, let us be very clear that we are looking for the physical equivalent of the **Ṛigvedic Sarasvatī and not for any sundry river bearing that name** or a name phonetically similar to that. Thus, it is necessary to recall the following hard facts from the *Ṛigveda* itself.

In the first place, as mentioned in Chapter I (above, pp.1-2), **the Ṛigvedic Sarasvatī lay *between* the Yamunā on the one hand and the Sutlej on the other (*imam me Gaṅge Yamune Sarasvatī Śutudri stomam sachatā Paruṣṇyā* ... *RV* 10.75.5). The names are mentioned serially in that text, from the Gaṅgā in the east to the Indus in the west, and this should leave no doubt in the mind of anyone about the geographical location of the Ṛigvedic Sarasvatī.**

Does the Harakhvati of the *Āvestā*, identified with modern Helmand in Afghanistan, foot the bill? Surely, not. There is no Yamunā or Sutlej in Afghanistan to sandwich the supposed Sarasvatī (Harakhvati)!

Secondly, as stated earlier (above, p.3), *RV* 3.23.4 mentions the **Dṛiṣadvatī and Āpayā as the tributaries of the Sarasvatī:**

Dṛiṣadvatyām mānuṣa Āpayāyām Sarasvatyām revadagne didīhi //

These two rivers are in Haryana (India) and not in Afghanistan. Are'nt they?

Thirdly, the **Ṛigvedic Sarasvatī is stated to have originated in the mountains and debouched in the ocean** (*RV* 7.95.2):

ekāchetat Sarasvatī nadīnām śuchir yatī giribhya ā samudrāt /

The Helmand of Afghanistan does not at all meet this requirement. It is far, far away from the ocean.

Fourthly, besides the above-mentioned geographical factors, there are some others which call for attention. For example, *RV*. 8.21.18 refers to a king Chitra as having lived on the bank of the Sarasvatī. Likewise, according to *RV*. 7.95.2 this river was associated with king Nahuṣa, and according to *RV*. 6.61.1 she gave Divodāsa, the famous Vedic king, to Vadhrayaśva. Again, *RV*. 6.61.12 shows that five specific 'peoples' lived in the Sarasvatī valley, of whom one has clearly been stated to have been the Pūrus vide *RV*. 7.96.2. **Is even one of these associations with the Sarasvatī vouchsafed by the Harakhvati of the *Āvestā*? If not, how can the claim of the Harakhvati to have been the Ṛigvedic Sarasvatī be upheld? There is no way!**

From the foregoing it must be abundantly clear that howsoever great the temptation to place the Ṛigvedic Sarasvatī in Afghanistan, it is just not possible to do so. No doubt the *Āvestā* does mention a river called the Harakhvati, but that can be explained if it is realized that the authors of the *Āvestā* and those of the *Ṛigveda* belonged to the same general stock and thus it should not surprise anybody if the names of some of the rivers in their respective regions are phonetically similar.

There is yet another erroneous view which calls for comments. In Verse *RV*. 2.41.16 the Sarasvatī has been addressed not only as '*ambitame*' (the best of mothers) and '*devitame*' (the best of goddesses) but also as '*nadītame*' (the best of rivers). Again, Verse *RV*.6.61.2 states that the Sarasvatī was capable of devastating the high ridges of the mountains on its banks through the force of its fast-moving and powerful currents (*iyam śuṣmebhir bisakhā ivārujat sānu girīṇām taviṣebhirūrmibhiḥ*). All this shows that the Sarasvatī was a mighty river. Since the present-day Sarasvatī is a small river, it has been argued that the Sarasvatī referred to in the *Ṛigveda* cannot be the present Sarasvatī. While dealing with the above-mentioned Verse 6.61.2, Griffith, in his translation of the *Ṛigveda* (1995 reprint, Vol. I, p.631), observes in a foot-note as follows:

> *She* : Sarasvatī as a river. The description given in the text can hardly apply to the small stream generally known under that name; and from this and other passages which will be noticed as they occur it seems probable that Sarasvatī is also another name of Sindhu or the Indus.

In this very footnote Griffith cites a reference to Zimmer to strengthen his viewpoint. Following faithfully these Western scholars, some Indian ones too uphold this view. For example, Irfan Habib and Faiz Habib (1991-92) state that there were three Sarasvatīs, the first one being the Helmand of Afghanistan, the second the Indus and the third the present-day Sarasvatī running through Haryana, Rajasthan, etc. While Griffith had a good knowledge of the Sanskrit language and was, therefore, within his rights to offer a view, howsoever tenuous, one really wonders at the performance of the Habibs.

Arguing their case for the Sarasvatī being the Helmand of Afghanistan, the Habibs state (ibid., 76).

> But it seems likely ...that Sarasvatī/Harakhvati was the name for the Helmand, above its junction with Arghandab. Otherwise it is difficult to understand how **Sarasvatī** could be put **between Sindhu and Sarayu**, i.e. the Indus and Hari-rud, as the major intervening river in *RV* X, 64.9.

It appears that the **Habibs have blindly followed Griffith's translation** of the hymn, which runs as follows:

Let the great streams come hither with their mighty help, Sindhu, Sarasvatī, and Sarayu with waves.

The fact is that the Ṛigvedic *text does not* put the Sarasvatī *between* the other two rivers. It reads:

***Sarasvatī Sarayuḥ Sindhurū**mibhir maho mahīravasā yantu vakṣaṇīḥ*

Hence the question of identifying the Sarasvatī with the Helmand on the basis of such a misconceived interpretation does not arise.

Earlier we have dealt *in extenso* with the issue why the Helmand of Afghanistan cannot be taken to be the Ṛigvedic Sarasvatī. The fact that **the Indus also cannot be identified with that Vedic river** is very clearly shown by the Ṛigvedic evidence itself. Whereas Verse 10.75.5 refers to the Sarasvatī as lying between the Yamunā and the Sutlej *(imam me Gaṅge Yamune Sarasvatī Śutudri ...)*, the very next Verse, viz. 10.75.6, not only mentions the Indus separately (**after** references to the Chenab, Jhelum, etc, in the former verse) but also refers to the tributaries that join it from the west, such as the Kurram, Gomal and Kabul (*Tṛiṣṭāmayā prathamam .... Tvam Sindho Kubhayā Gomatīm Krumum Mehatnvā saratham yābhirīyase*). **Can we afford to ignore the categorical evidence provided by these two adjacent verses? Surely not, unless we blindfold ourselves under a spell of bigotry**.

(II) THE CORRECT IDENTIFICATION, BASED ON A CORRELATION BETWEEN THE ṚIGVEDIC GEOGRAPHY AND GROUND REALITIES

Anyway, letting Sharma and Habibs bask in their self-glory, the question that has to be squarely answered is: If the Helmand and Indus were not the Ṛigvedic Sarasvatī, which other river can lay its claim to being so and why? To answer this question we must, even at the cost of repetition, once again return to the geographic data provided by the *Ṛigveda* itself.

In the first place, as the text says (*RV*. 10.75.5, above, pp.1-2), the Sarasvatī lay between the Yamunā and the Sutlej. Today there is a river called the Sarasvatī which runs between the just-mentioned two rivers and thus fulfils the first condition. It originates at the foot of the Siwaliks and flows southwestwards in Haryana where it passes by the towns of Pipli, Kurukshetra and Pehowa, after which it joins the Ghaggar. This combined stream proceeds further down but dries up near Sirsa. Thereafter only its dry bed can be identified. It continues further southwestwards and is called the Ghaggar in northern Rajasthan. Further down, it goes by the name of the Hakra in the Cholistan region of Pakistan. Thereafter it turns southwards and in Sindh its branches are variously called the Raini, Wahinda and Nara. Finally, as the available evidence suggests, it fell into the Rann of Kachchh.

Secondly, the *Ṛigveda* (3.23.4) mentions the Dṛiṣadvatī as being one of the tributaries of the Sarasvatī. And this is precisely so in the case of the Sarasvatī–Ghaggar combine we have just referred to. The Dṛiṣadvatī, also now dry like the Sarasvatī, has been identified with the modern Chautang. Passing by the towns of Bhadra, Nohar, etc., it joins the Sarasvatī–Ghaggar combine near Suratgarh. Thus, the present-day Sarasvatī–Ghaggar fulfils the second criterion also.

In this context it may be well worthwhile to quote from a paper by Yash Pal *et al.* (1984) which is based on a critical study of Landsat imagery of the Ghaggar–Sarasvatī basin (pls. 214 and 215 of their paper; of these, the former is reproduced here as Fig. 2.1). These experts have also produced an integrated map showing the march of the Sarasvatī–Ghaggar combine, along with the ancient beds of the Śutudri (Sutlej) and the Dṛiṣadvatī (modern Chautang) which fed it (ibid., fig. 49.1). They observe (ibid.: 495):

(i) The ancient bed of the Ghaggar has a constant width of about 6 to 8 km from Shatrana in Punjab to Marot in Pakistan (figs 49.1 and 2). The bed stands out very clearly having a dark tone in the black-and-white imagery and reddish one in false colour composites.

(ii) There is a clear palaeo-channel southeast of the river Markanda which joins the ancient bed of the Ghaggar near Shatrana Channel Y1 (1 and 2). The present Sarasvatī mostly flows through this channel.

(iii) Another channel, Y2, which corresponds to the present Chautang, seems to join the Ghaggar near Suratgarh (fig. 49.1).

Referring to the relationship between the Sarasvatī and the Sutlej the authors state (ibid.: 494):

> Our studies thus show that the Satluj was the main tributary of the Ghaggar and that subsequently the tectonic movements may have forced the Satluj westward and the Ghaggar dried.

These experts finally conclude (ibid.: 497):

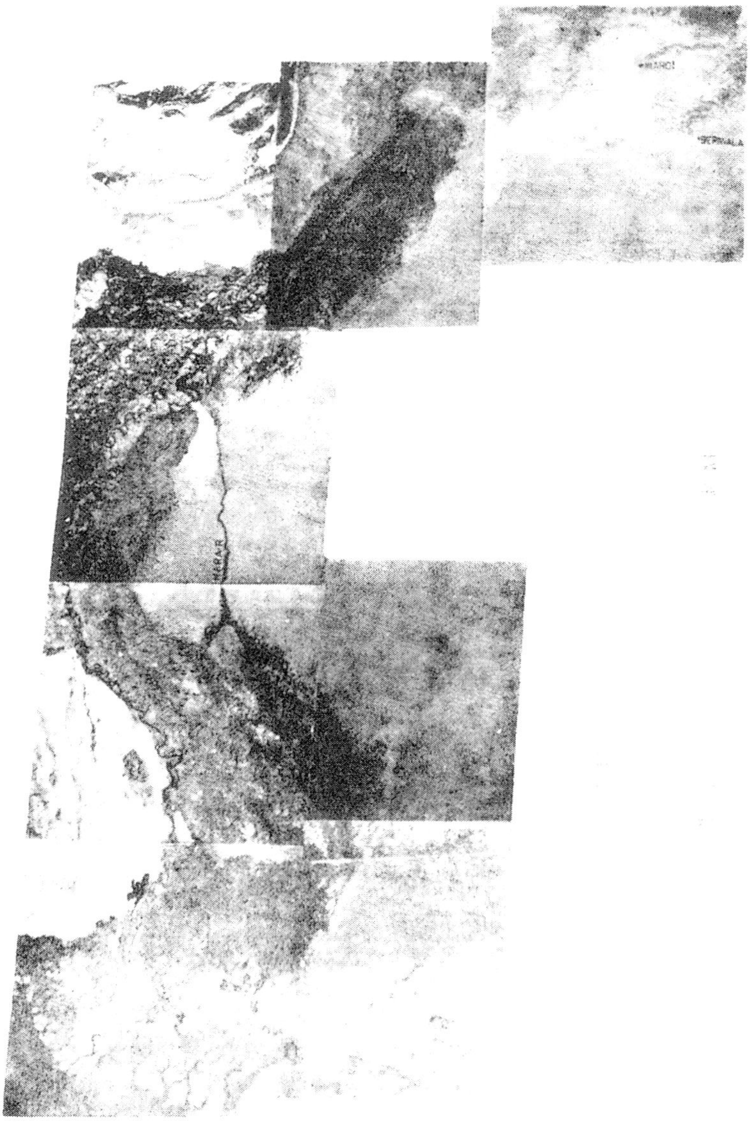

Fig. 2.1 Synoptic view of the lower Indus valley, showing the possible course of the Sarasvatī beyond Marot through the Nara into the Rann of Kachchh. The Rann is conspicuous because of the high reflectance (white tone) of its encrustation

Palaeo-environmental changes in the northwestern subcontinent have been caused by climatic, tectonic and anthropogenic factors. Tectonic factors assumed such overwhelming importance only because the major channels like those of the Sarasvatī were structurally controlled by enechelon faults. It was because of this reason that even relatively minor tectonic movements caused considerable changes in the configuration of the palaeo-channels. The distribution of the archaeological sites was also determined by the vagrancy of these rivers.

As discussed above, during the period 4-5 millennia B.P. northwestern Rajasthan was a much greener place with the Sarasvatī flowing through it. **Some of the present rivers joined to make the Sarasvatī a mighty river which probably discharged into the sea (Rann of Kutch) through the Nara, *without* joining the Indus.**

In so far as the lower Sindh region is concerned, further attention may be drawn to a recent (1999) paper by Louis Flam. He observes as follows (p. 58):

> Southwest of Fort Derawar, east of Rahimyar Khan, the Hakra Course becomes increasingly unclear and intermittently becomes 'lost' beneath the sand dunes which have encroached upon the area. Remnants of the Hakra's course re-emerge where dunes are less numerous. From Fort Derawar to the south, the Hakra can be aligned with the Raini and Wahinda remnants, which subsequently connect with and blend into the Nara channel.

He then concludes (p. 65; see also his Fig. 20, here Fig. 2.2):

> The Sindhu Nadi has been recognized in this study as the former course of the Indus River during the greater parts of the fourth and third millennia B.C. The Sindhu Nadi has been traced in the northwestern, central and southeastern portions of the Lower Indus Basin from remnants visible on aerial photo composites and confirmed by ground observations.
>
> In addition to the Sindhu Nadi, **the Nara Nadi has been recognized as an exclusive perennial river which flowed in the northeastern, east-central and southeastern portions of the Lower Indus Basin during the fourth and third millennia B.C.** Traces of the Sindhu Nadi and the Nara Nadi indicate that in the southeastern portion of the Lower Indus Basin the two rivers formed a confluence and flowed as one river in the area south of the present-day town of Naukot. Available evidence suggests that during the fourth and third millennia the delta of the combined Sindhu Nadi and Nara Nadi was located near the Rann of Kachchh on the eastern side of the Lower Indus Basin to somewhere between Hyderabad and Thatta in Sindh.

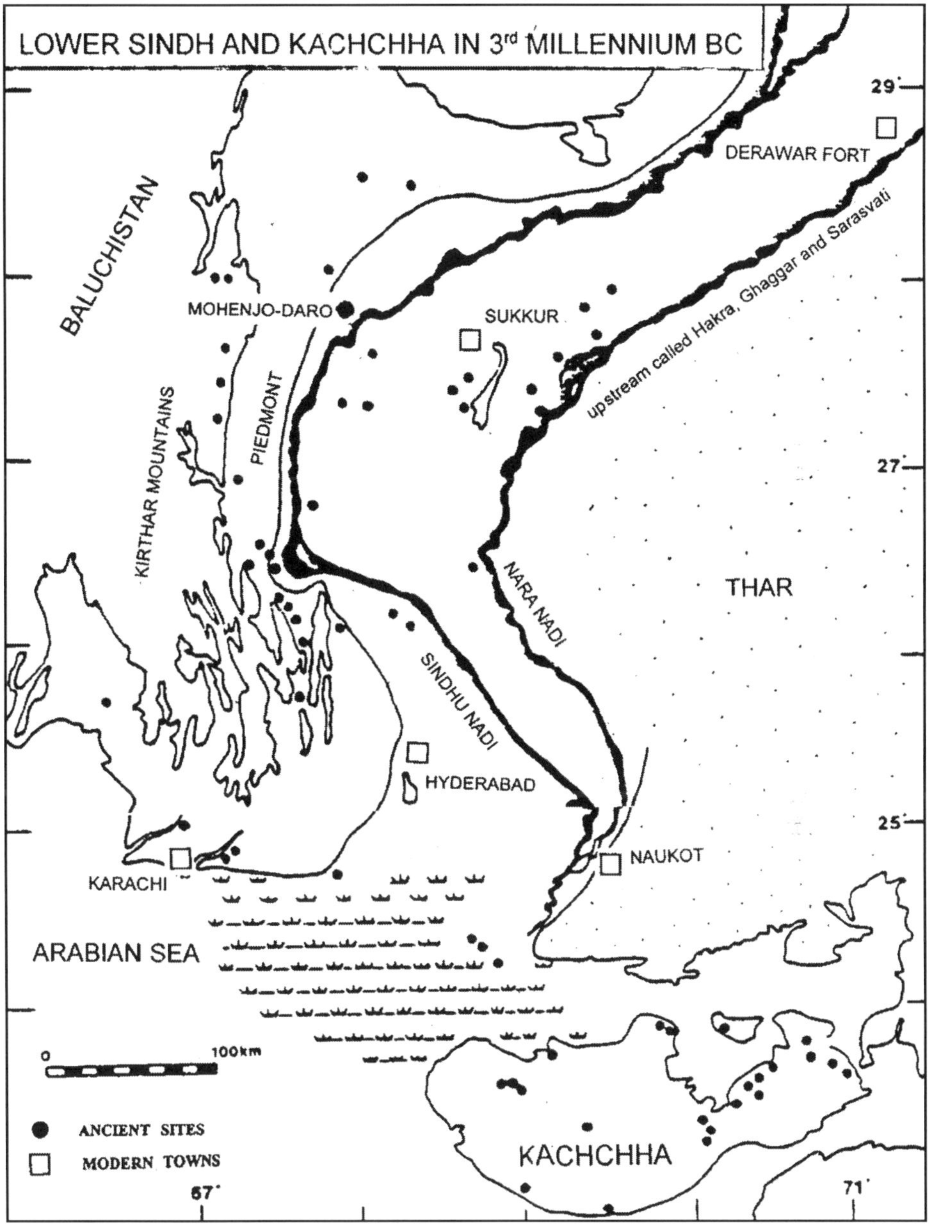

Fig. 2.2 Lower Sindh and Kachchh in the 3rd millennium BC

The foregoing statements made by various experts, after a very careful study of the aerial and ground data, should leave no doubt in anybody's mind that the now-dry Sarasvatī, which in its westward and southward courses is now known successively as the Ghaggar, Hakra, Raini, Wahinda and Nara, was in the fourth-third millennia BC a mighty river, going all the way down to the sea (*yatī giribhya ā samudrāt* of the *Ṛigveda*).

(III) THE SOURCE AND PERENNIAL WATER-SUPPLY

The third diagnostic feature referred to in the *Ṛigveda* (7.95.2), as already mentioned, is that the Sarasvatī originated in the mountains and went all the way down to the sea. That the present-day Sarasvatī–Ghaggar combine finally joined the sea has already been shown above. The only question that now remains to be answered is: Did the Sarasvatī originate in the mountains (i.e. the Himalayas) and not just start off as a seasonal stream at the foot of the Siwaliks, as it does now?

In this context attention may be invited to an excellent paper on the topic by two eminent geologists, V.M.K. Puri and B.C. Verma (1998). This paper is replete with highly scientific data and other details which are useful in their own way but would be rather burdensome for the readers of the present book. Hence we give below only the essentials. (Those interested in further details are advised to go to the original paper.)

A detailed survey of the mountainous region lying between the Yamunā and the Markanda rivers has revealed four terraces which have been labelled as T_0, T_1, T_2 and T_3 from the top downwards. Remnants of the terrace T_0, identified about 2 km south-southeast of Sudanwala, rise to a height of 660 m above the mean sea level (MSL). The most noteworthy point about this terrace is that it contains, besides other material, pebbles of quartzite and metamorphic rocks. Similar high terraces (T_0 and T_1) and with almost identical lithological composition have also been identified in the area. However, it has been noted that the lower (and, therefore, younger) terraces, viz. T_2 and T_3, in these valleys are completely bereft of the kind of material found in the uppermost two terraces, except along the present-day Yamunā course. After a thorough analysis of the evidence provided by the various terraces and their lithology, these experts conclude (ibid.: 16):

> Thus, the terraces studied in Sudanwala, Bata, Garibnath and Markanda provide

an irrefutable geological evidence to suggest a course of a river that was flowing in almost west-northwesterly direction in the past. Its dimension was very large as it contained a very high discharge that traversed in its upper reaches a terrain of quartzite and metamorphic rocks. Such a region does exist in central and upper reaches of Yamunā fourth order basin where Central Crystallines and Jutogh group of rocks are located towards north, north-east and eastern side of above-mentioned four terraces. Moreover, in the Paonta valley, there is a clear evidence that **prior to the present Yamunā river, there existed a major river channel at a much higher elevation that followed a westerly and southwesterly course through a route now almost completely obliterated on Siwalik platform due to erosion but its terraces are still observed along Adh Badrī-Markanda link in the plains immediately to the south of Siwalik belt.**

Looking further up for the 'source' of this mighty river which is now 'lost', one's attention is naturally drawn to the basin of the Tons where quartzite and metamorphic rocks dominate. **'All the evidences', Puri and Verma thus affirm, 'point to only one conclusion that the present-day Tons was in fact Vedic Saraswati in its upper reaches'.** (ibid.: 16)

The tremendous amount of water that the Tons and other rivers receive must have come from glaciers. These scientists have produced an excellent map (ibid. Fig. 8; here Fig. 2.3) which shows that the Vedic Sarasvatī was the ultimate outflow from a combination of glaciers which included, amongst others, the ones known as the Sarasvatī, Jamadar and Supin glaciers. It was near Naitwar that these glaciers finally melted to form the river.

Moving first in a southwesterly direction and then in a westerly one, the Vedic Sarasvatī finally broke through the Siwaliks at Adh Badri and descended on the plains (Puri and Verma, ibid., Fig. 9; here Fig. 2.4). The story of the subsequent course of the Sarasvatī (combined with the Ghaggar) has been detailed earlier and needs no repetition.

The origin of the Vedic Sarasvatī from the glaciers in the Himalayas, which made it a perennial river on its own, and its being joined by the Sutlej from the northwest, indeed made it a formidable river. This is clearly indicated by its bed, though now dry, which was as much as 6-8 kilometres in width for quite some part of its length. And it is this might that is reflected when the Ṛigvedic seers sang:

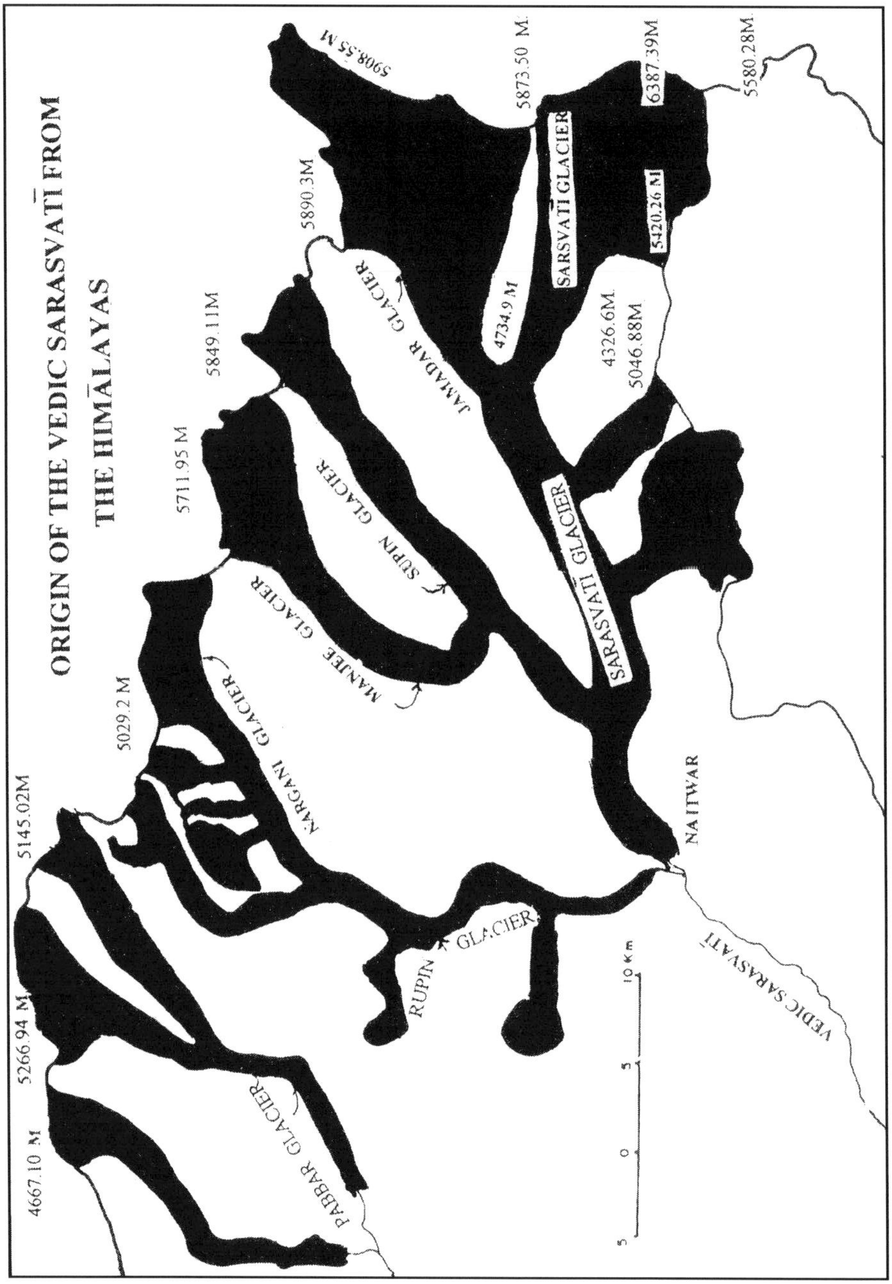

Fig. 2.3 Origin of the Vedic Sarasvatī from the Himalayas

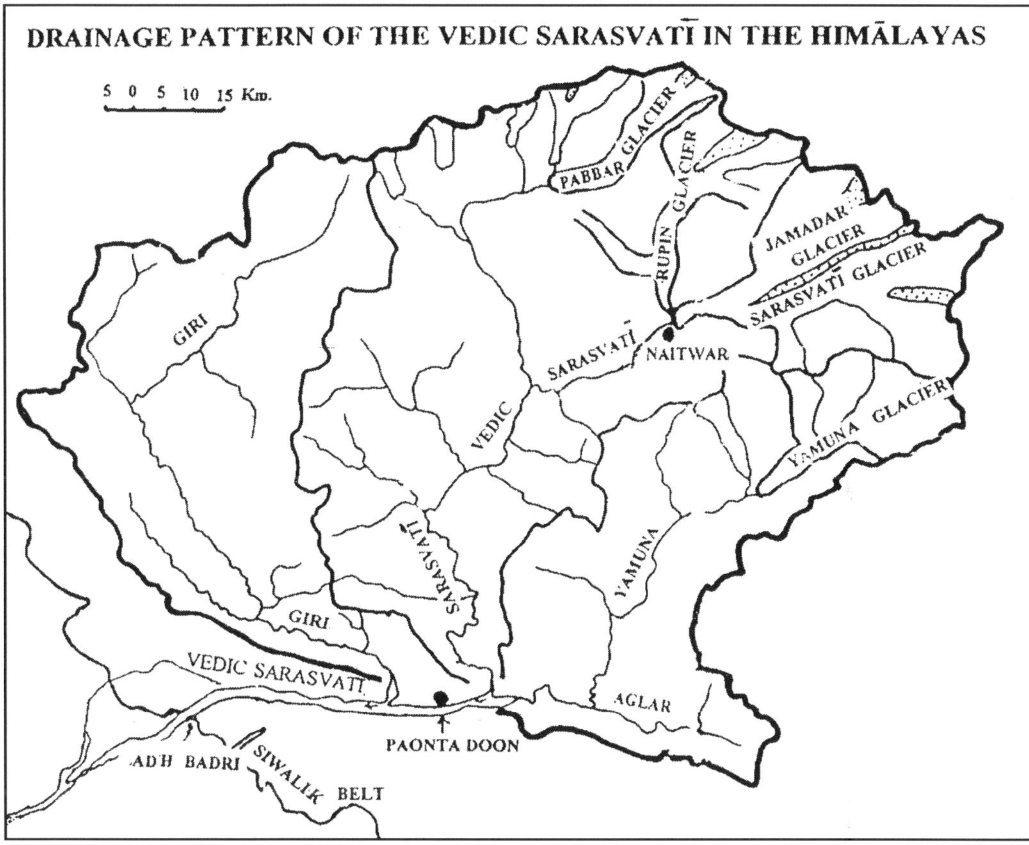

Fig. 2.4 Drainage Pattern of the Vedic Sarasvatī in the Himalayas

Iyam śuṣmebhir bisakhā ivārujat sānu girīṇām taviṣebhirūrmibhiḥ (6.61.2)

This (Sarasvatī) has shattered the mountain peaks with her fast and powerful waves, or

Ekāchetat Sarasvatī nadīnām śuchir yatī giribhya ā samudrāt (7.95.2)

Purest among all the rivers and vibrant, the Sarasvatī moves on from the mountains to the ocean.

Based on the data discussed above, a map is drawn of the courses of the Sarasvatī and its principal tributaries in the Haryana, Panjab, Rajasthan and Cholistan region during the third millennium BC. On this map are also

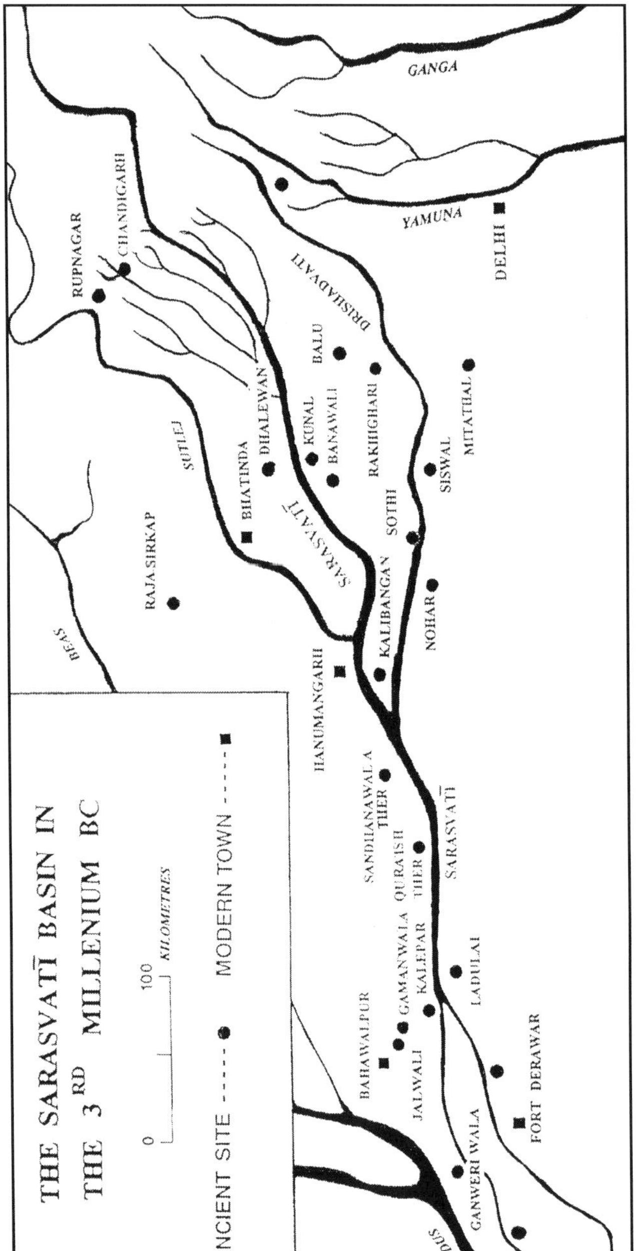

Fig. 2.5 The Sarasvatī Basin in the 3rd Millennium BC

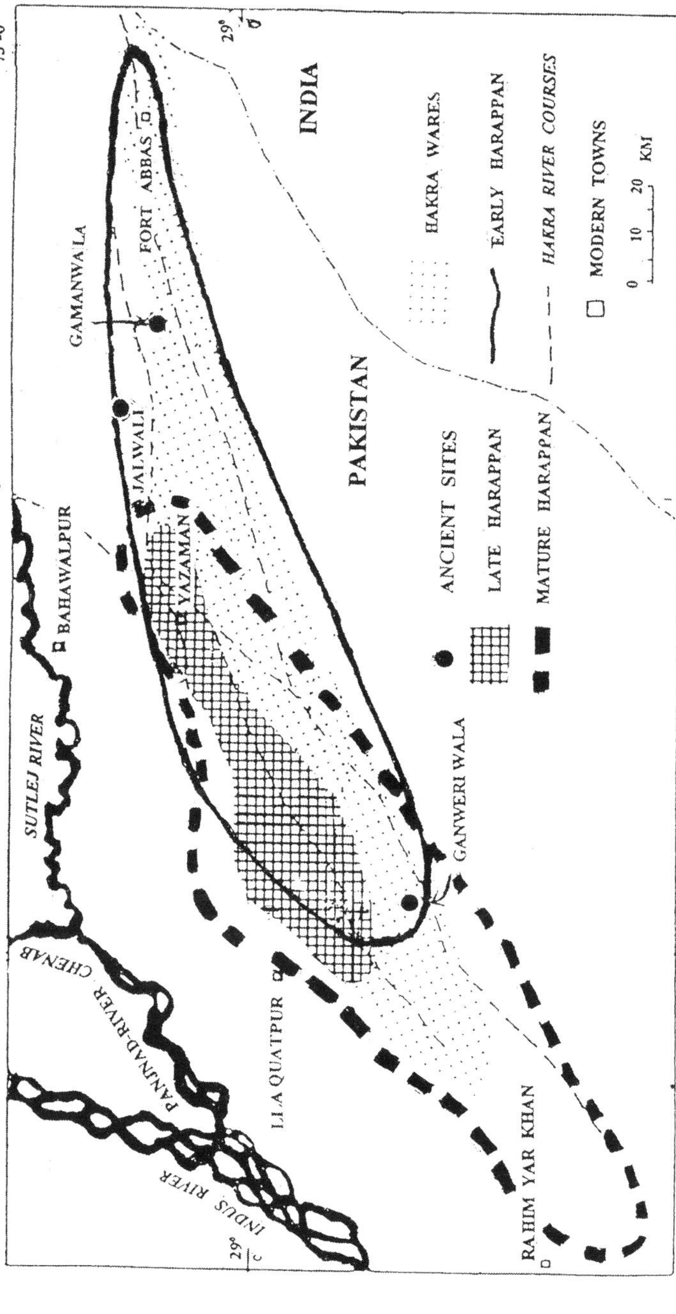

Fig. 2.6 Areas of Hakra Ware and Early, Mature and Late Harappan Sites

plotted some of the more noteworthy sites of the Early and Mature Harappan times (Fig. 2.5). A separate and detailed map (Fig. 2.6) is also given of the ancient sites of various categories in the Sarasvatī (Hakra) basin in Cholistan (after Mughal 1992).

(IV) WHEN AND HOW DID THE SARASVATĪ DRY UP?

But when and how did such a mighty river stop flowing, leaving behind only a sand-and-silt bed on the terra firma and its memory through literature and folklore?

The first query, namely 'when', can be easily answered on the basis of archaeological data and radiocarbon dates. The Mature Harappan settlement at Kalibangan, located on the bank of the ancient Sarasvatī (now going by the name of the Ghaggar), had to be abandoned because of the drying up of the river that was once its life-giver. Radiocarbon dates clearly indicate that Kalibangan came to an end around 1900 BC (Lal 1997: 245). And since the site had to be abandoned because of the stoppage of water-supply from the adjacent Sarasvatī river, it follows that the river dried up some time at the beginning of the second millennium BC.

The Vedic literature clearly refers to the drying up of the Sarasvatī. For example, the *Pañchviṁśa Brāhmaṇa* (XXV.10.16) states: 'At a distance of a journey of forty days on horseback from the spot where the Sarasvatī is lost (in the sands of the desert), (is situated) Plakṣa Prāsravaṇa' (Caland's translation, 1931, reprint 1982, p.636).

While it may not be easy to estimate correctly the distance involved in the forty-day horseback journey and thus to identify the exact place where the Sarasvatī disappeared, it is nevertheless clear that by the time of the *Pañchaviṁśa Brāhmaṇa* the river had dried up.

Though not quite germane to the present theme of the book, it would be seen that since the Sarasvatī has been described as a mighty flowing river in the *Ṛigveda* and the above-mentioned archaeological-cum-radiocarbon evidence shows that the Sarasvatī dried up around 1900 BC, **the *Ṛigveda* has got to be anterior to that date. By how many centuries? It is anyone's guess.**

We may now pass on to the second query raised earlier, viz. that of 'how?' To look for the factors that contributed to the disappearance of such a mighty river as the Sarasvatī we have once again to refer to the excellent evidence

Fig. 2.7 Appearance of Bata-Markanda Divide

marshalled by Puri and Verma in the aforementioned paper. During the life-time of the Vedic Sarasvatī there was a major seismic activity, as a result of which there came up the Bata-Markanda Divide, which is nearly 30 m in height (Fig. 13 of Puri and Verma; here Fig. 2.7). The net result was that the Sarasvatī could no longer flow westwards into the Adh Badri opening, but had to reverse its direction to the east. And since not far off there was the Yamunā Tear opening, it provided another drainage. The mighty Sarasvatī met her end at the hands of the Seismic Demon which, as if, throttled her by the Bata-Markanda Divide and forced her out through the Yamunā Tear. The Himalayan-glacier-fed, perennial Sarasvatī having died out, what survived was a rain-fed seasonal stream, starting off from the Siwalik foothills.

CHAPTER III

THE MOST ANCIENT CIVILIZATION OF THE SARASVATĪ VALLEY

(I) INTRODUCTORY

As late as 1920, it was believed by most Western scholars that India had no civilization worth the name before the invasion of Alexander in 326 BC. This was the scenario in spite of the fact that there did exist the *Veda*s which, even on a conservative estimate of Max Muller, were at least as old as 1200 BC. However, no one could ever dream of the unknown treasures the Mother Earth had in her womb. Thus, the very next year (1921) she sprang a big surprise when she delivered to the spade of Daya Ram Sahni, at Harappa in Panjab, the remains of an altogether unknown ancient civilization. This was immediately (1922) followed by a similar delivery at Mohenjo-daro in Sindh, to R.D. Banerjee. The archaeological remains so discovered completely belied the above-mentioned common belief and straightaway took back the antiquity of Indian civilization by more than 2,000 years. These initial discoveries were followed by full-fledged excavations at Mohenjo-daro by John Marshall (1931) and at Harappa by M.S. Vats (1940), which established that this newly identified Indian civilization was not only as old as the contemporary civilizations of Egypt and Iraq but in some ways even excelled them. For example, the Indian cities were regularly planned, with the streets oriented north-south and east-west, whereas no such planning existed in either of the two civilizations just named. The use of kiln-fired bricks was another innovation by the Indians. There is a long list of Indian excellence that one can produce, but here it may suffice to refer just to the superbly carved steatite seals, hardly 3 x 3 cm in size but depicting intricate scenes or individual deities or animals, the like of which were never produced in the contemporary world.

But the wheel of fortune always keeps on going up and down. In 1947 the country was partitioned and all the sites of this civilization went over to

Pakistan, excepting two very tiny ones, viz. Kotla Nihang in Panjab and Rangpur in Gujarat, whose antiquity was also debated. Indian archaeologists, however, took up the challenge and it is no exaggeration to say that today India has more sites (nearing a thousand), associated with the various stages — early, middle and late — of this civilization, than has Pakistan. But the number is hardly that matters. What is more important is that these Indian sites have added new dimensions to our knowledge of this hoary civilization. For example, India has given to the world the earliest dockyard known to humanity. Discovered at Lothal, in Gujarat, it dates back to the middle of the third millennium BC (Rao 1979). Another earliest, assignable to the first quarter of that very millennium, is a ploughed agricultural field, discovered at Kalibangan in Rajasthan (Lal 1970-71). Dholavira, in Gujarat, has given a unique plan of the settlement, comprising a Citadel, a Middle Town and a Lower Town (Bisht 1994). Another noteworthy site in the same region is Surkotada (Joshi 1990).

In recent years a lot has been written about the Harappan Civilization (Lal 1997; Kenoyer 1998; and Possehl 1999). Hence it is not considered necessary to go into those details here. However, since this book deals specially with the Sarasvatī valley, it would be well worthwhile to highlight some of the special features pertaining to the sites located in this region.

(II) ITS ADOLESCENCE

As stated in earlier chapters, the bed of the ancient Sarasvatī is known by various names, from the Himalayan region to the sea. In Haryana, it joins the Ghaggar, after which it goes by the latter name all through Haryana and Rajasthan. On entering the Cholistan region of Pakistan, it is called the Hakra. Later on it turns southwards and in Sindh it goes by several names, such as the Raini, Wahinda and Nara. Since no worthwhile archaeological fieldwork has been carried out along the beds of these last-named channels, it is difficult to say much about the sites that may have existed on their banks in antiquity.

However, Mughal's work in Cholistan has brought to light very valuable data (Mughal 1992 and 1997; here Fig. 2.6). It is estimated that the earliest settlements in this region go back to the second half of the fourth millennium BC. The cultural assemblage encountered at these sites has been given the name of Hakra Culture, after the name of the river itself. Of it, as many as 99 sites have been identified. In terms of technological development, the Hakra Culture seems to have moved out of the neolithic stage, but does not seem yet to have attained full-fledged Bronze Age status. Only sporadic bits of copper are recorded, though at the same time it must be admitted that the material comes only from surface-exploration since no excavation has been carried out at any of the sites. The assemblage included lithic tools like scrapers, borers, parallel-sided blades, often retouched, and leaf-shaped arrowheads, the last-named being reminiscent of an early tradition. Also present were stone grinders, possibly used for grinding cereals, although no grains as such were collected. Amongst other antiquities from this complex mention may be made of terracotta figurines of bulls, characterized by their conjoined legs, again an early feature. Terracotta bangles indicated how the womenfolk bedecked themselves. Thus, on the whole the economic level cannot be regarded as high. Nevertheless, the pottery showed quite some varieties. It was handmade as well as wheel-turned but in both cases fired under oxidizing conditions so as to turn red. However, the external features deserve notice since some of these persisted in the subsequent cultural stages. Some pots were characterized by an exterior coating of mud intermixed with small bits of pottery. This tradition goes back to IA levels of Amri in Sindh, where it may be ascribed to the earlier part of the fourth millennium BC. In another category were pots with incised designs on the exterior. These comprised groups of lines, placed in a horizontal or vertical or curvilinear fashion. Some of the pots, made of fine fabric and covered with a red or chocolate slip, bore broad bands in black colour along the neck and/or shoulder. In a few cases even the entire exterior of the pots was covered with a black slip. The pottery has been described here in some detail since many of these features continued for some time into the next cultural stage called the Early Harappan.

Of the Early Harappan stage, Mughal records only 40 sites (as against 99 of the Hakra stage). This lesser number does not seem to be due to any demographic diminution. The reason is that whereas the 'Hakra' settlements were very shallow, indicative of the fact that the occupants freely moved from one site to another, the Early Harappans had become more sedentary. Thus, not only was the cultural deposit at the Early Harappan sites thicker but the sites also covered much larger area. In fact, the size-factor has a lot to tell us beyond the mere figures. To put the facts first. While about half of the Early Harappan settlements were below 5 hectares in size and one-fourth between 5 and 10 hectares, the remaining one-fourth covered an area more than 10 hectares. More importantly, some of the settlements were very much larger: for example, Jalwali was 22.5 hectares and Gamanwala even more, viz. 27.3 hectares. This clearly demonstrates that amidst smaller villages, larger towns had also begun to grow up and it is not unlikely that these bigger towns may have started dominating the smaller ones around them, thus sowing the seeds of some kind of power-structure — may be of chiefdom, for all one may guess.

Not only were these Early Harappan settlements bigger in size, but they had also begun to show some specialized features. Mughal records that many of them had an 'industrial component', besides, of course, the usual habitation area. Since, as already stated, no site in Cholistan has been excavated and we have, on the other hand, many sites in the upstream area of the Hakra-Ghaggar-Sarasvatī valley which have undergone operations of the spade, it is proposed to deal with the features of the Early Harappan Culture, as gleaned from the upstream sites. However, to complete the story of the Cholistan region, it may suffice here to state that during the Mature Harappan times the number of sites rose to 174, of which one, named Ganweriwala, was as much as 81.5 hectares in size. The number dwindled to 50 in the Late Harappan times. The implication of these numbers will be discussed later when we deal with the effect of the dessication of the Sarasvatī on the demography of the region.

Though there are many important and well excavated Early Harappan and Mature Harappan sites as we proceed upstream from the Cholistan region, for example Kalibangan, Banawali and Rakhigarhi, we propose moving straight on to Kunal (cf. Fig. 2.5), located in district Hissar, Haryana, since at that site there was hardly any later overload to have stood in the way of horizontal excavation of the earlier levels. The result is that here we have a somewhat detailed picture of the Early Harappan Culture (Khatri and Acharya 1995).

Though small in expanse, covering an area of only about 1.2 hectares, Kunal has a vertical deposit of over 3 metres. Within it, the excavators have identified three Sub-periods, designated as Ia, Ib and Ic, from bottom upwards. While on the one hand these throw light on the evolutionary changes within the Early Harappan occupation itself, on the other, they have yielded a good deal of material which contributed to the formation of the Mature Harappan Culture.

Finding that the land at Kunal was uneven, the first occupants of the site

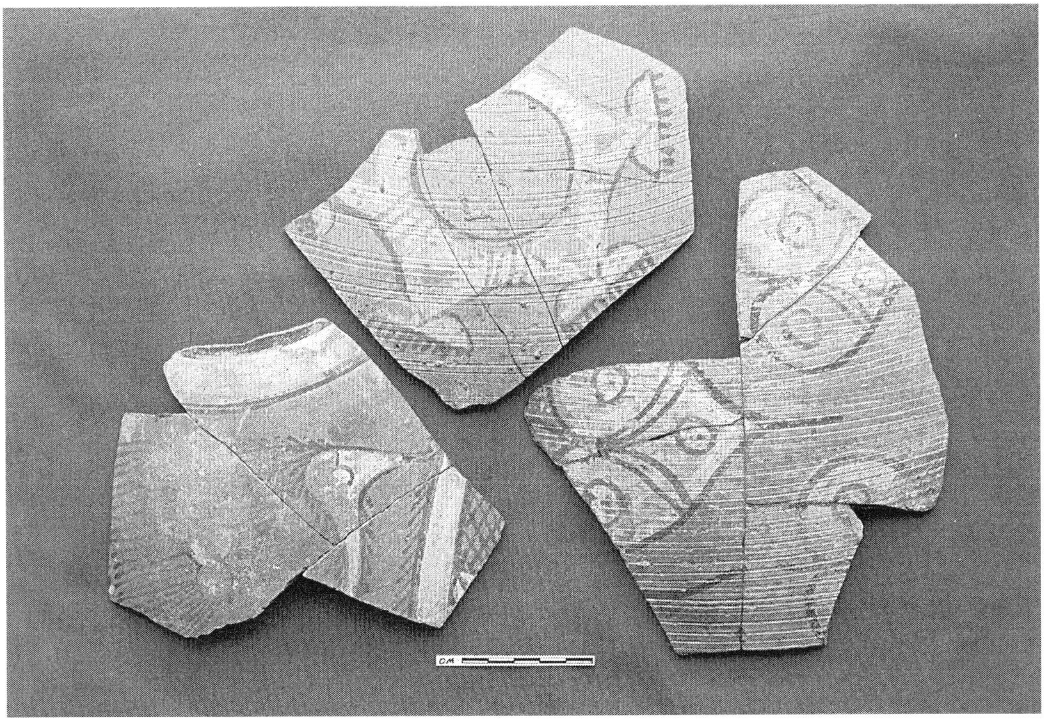

Fig. 3.1 Kunal: Pottery, painted with two colours: black outline and white in-filling. Early Harappan

(Sub-period Ia) levelled it up with kankary red soil, collected from the neighbouring areas. However, they did not build their houses above the ground-level, but excavated pits as their dwellings. Maybe they wanted to protect themselves from the northerly cold winds to which the region is exposed. Or maybe they just carried on with a tradition which they inherited from their forefathers, whose settlements, however, we have yet to identify in the region. Be that as it may, the pits were circular on plan, with a diameter of about 2 metres. The depth ranged in the neighbourhood of a metre. These pits were provided with a shed over them, as indicated by the remains of post-holes along the periphery. Although these early Kunalians were still using stone and bone tools, they had well moved into a Copper Age, as testified to by the presence of fish-hooks and arrow-heads of that metal. Their technical skill is also indicated by micro-beads of chalcedony. However, particular attention may be drawn to the pottery used by these inhabitants. Besides the

Hakra Ware, the details of which have been given earlier, the Kunalians used a red ware which carried on its exterior painted designs in two colours. The outline was usually in black, while the space within was filled in with white. The use of these two colours is a very distinctive feature of the Early Harappan pottery not only in the entire Sarasvatī valley but also much beyond it, as far south-west as Sindh and as far north-west as the North West Frontier Province, both in Pakistan.

As time passed, the size of the pits also increased, perhaps to accommodate the extended family. In Sub-period Ib, these were found to be up to 3 metres in diameter. There is also evidence, in the form of mud-brick hearths, of cooking having been done within the pits. Further, to strengthen the sides, the pits were provided with mud-brick lining. In this sub-period the Hakra Ware was on the wane, and the bichrome ware increased. Fig. 3.1 illustrates three potsherds in this ware, which are noteworthy for their designs. In this context, it needs to be emphasized that the peacock and pipal-leaf designs, originating in these Early Harappan levels, became very characteristic amongst the designs on the Mature Harappan pottery. Besides the painted designs there were certain pottery-shapes, e.g. jars and beakers in a sturdy red ware, which anticipated their counterparts in the upcoming Mature stage. Also must be noted from these levels terracotta 'cakes' which, again, are so distinctive an element of the Mature Harappa Culture.

Sub-period Ic ushered in some more novelties. The pits gave way to over-ground houses, which were either square or rectangular on plan. However, no less remarkable was the fact that the bricks used in the construction of these houses were in the ratio of 4:2:1, in respect of their length: breadth: thickness. This, it must be noted, was another characteristic feature of the Harappan Civilization at its maturity. During Sub-period Ic grain-production had also gone up, as suggested by the presence of silos. These were circular on plan and were plastered with lime and clay, perhaps to safeguard the contents against insects. Such silos have also been found in the Early Harappan levels at Kalibangan, a site to which we shall refer in some detail shortly.

The affluence of these Early Harappans of Kunal is vouchsafed not only by surplus food-production, to which a reference has already been made, but also by a variety of objects in metals — copper, silver and gold — besides beads of many semi-precious stones. Of copper, the objects included fish-hooks, axes, inverted V-shaped arrow-heads, spearheads and ornaments like coiled finger-rings and coiled cones. It needs to be added that many of these types continued into the Mature Harappan times. Whatever may have been the source for procuring the raw material — perhaps the Khetri mines, as seems to have been the case during the Mature Harappan times as well — it is clear that the actual manufacturing was done at Kunal itself. This is established by the discovery at the site of a crucible to which molten copper was still sticking.

In one of the houses were discovered a large number of silver and gold beads. While some of these were barrel-shaped or cup-shaped, particular interest attaches to the discular ones of silver, with the threading-perforation being along the diameter (see Fig. 4.5). Similar beads have been found in the Mature Harappan levels at Lothal (see Fig. 4.6), though in the latter case the metal used was gold. Anyway, the origin of the type is clearly Early Harappan. While speaking of beads, mention must be made that some of them were made of faience, lapis lazuli and carnelian. In most cases the raw material had to be brought from elsewhere, but the use of lapis lazuli is particularly significant, since it had to be imported from as far away as Afghanistan or Baluchistan. This at once points to long-distance trade. In this context it needs to be added that Kunal has also yielded seals, six of steatite and one of shell, which apparently were used for sealing traded commodities. Like their Mature Harappan successors, the steatite seals of Kunal are square in shape and have a perforated knob at the back. However, the engraved designs on the obverse are simple geometric motifs, and not the animal or human ones so typical of the Harappan specimens. Also wanting in the Kunal examples are the inscriptions. One wonders if writing was actually used during the Early Harappan times, although Kunal and like it many Early Harappan sites have yielded graffiti which may be regarded as the forerunners of many of the Mature Harappan signs (Lal 1992).

At what socio-political level the inhabitants of Kunal stood, it is difficult to determine categorically. However, it would be well worthwhile to refer here to the discovery, from within a pot in a large-sized house, of many silver ornaments wrapped in a silver sheet. As the excavators state (Khatri and Acharya 1995: 86), the lot consisted of 'two tiaras, one small and one large, each with a large fully opened flower having petals topped with a decoration like the Greek letter alpha' (Fig. 3.2). The collection also included a multi-

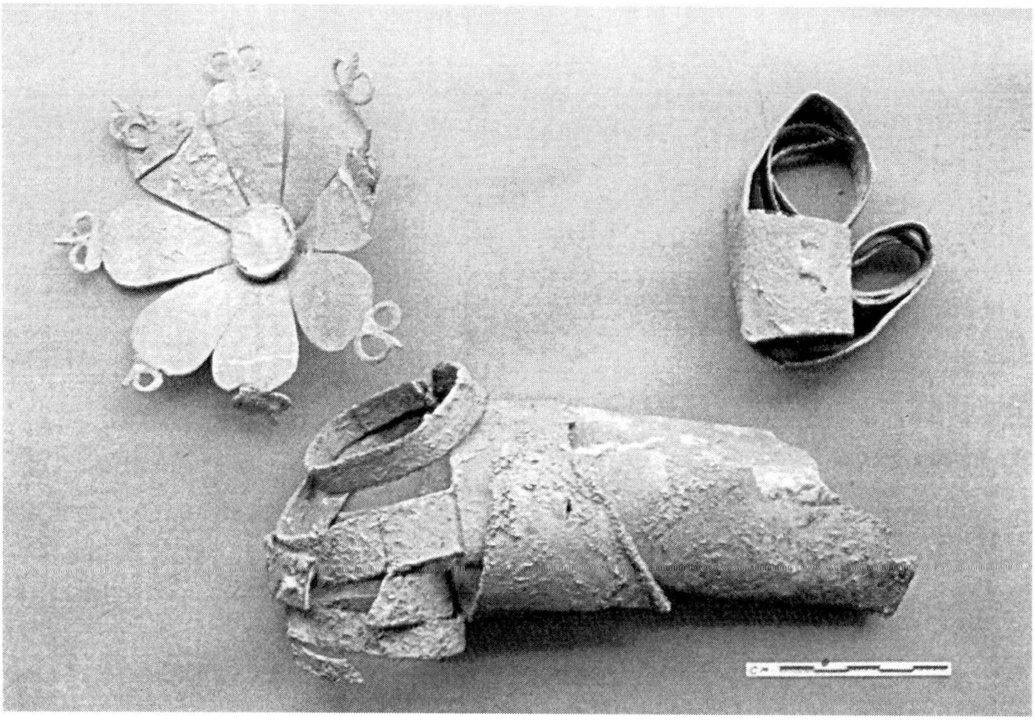

Fig. 3.2 Kunal: Silver ornaments. Early Harappan

spiralled armlet of silver (Fig. 4.8), reminding us of similar ornaments bedecking the arms of the famous 'dancing girl' from Mohenjo-daro (see Fig. 4.7). This outstanding hoard sets one thinking about the socio-economic level of the house-owner concerned. Evidently, he was no mere commoner, and it has been surmised, perhaps rightly, that he was someone special, maybe the chief of the settlement. Of course, in the present stage of our knowledge of the Early Harappan set-up, this will remain no more than a guess.

How far in antiquity does the settlement at Kunal go back? There are only three radiocarbon dates for the site, which place it between ca. 3016 and 2577 BC. Since no sample from the earliest level seems to have been dated, it is not unlikely that the first settlement at Kunal may have begun some time in the last quarter of the fourth millennium BC. The closing date for Kunal seems to be in order, since, as we shall see later, the Mature Harappan stage ushered in around 2600 BC.

We now propose to get back once again downstream on the Sarasvatī, east of Cholistan, and take up the site of Kalibangan, located on the left bank of the now-dry river, in District Hanumangarh, Rajasthan. Altogether, there are three mounds, of which the one in the middle (named KLB-2) is the largest and highest, that on its west (KLB-1) smaller and less in height, while the one on the extreme east (KLB-3) is the smallest (see Fig. 3.10). The overall periphery of the site is about 1.5-2 kilometres, and the highest point (on the middle mound) is about 10 metres above the surrounding ground-level. The middle and easternmost mounds have yielded the remains of Mature Harappa Culture, but the westernmost mound (KLB-1) was occupied during both Early and Mature Harappan times, with some time-interval in between.

Because of the thick Mature Harappan deposits in the central part of KLB-1, only a limited portion of the Early Harappan levels could be exposed, mostly in the peripheral regions where the overlying Mature Harappan strata had been denuded over the past four millennia. Nevertheless quite a few significant features of the Early Harappan settlement were noticed. In the first place, it must be stated that, unlike Kunal, the Early Harappan settlement at Kalibangan was duly fortified — a feature also shared by Banawali, to be discussed later. (In this context it may perhaps be also added that outside the Sarasvatī valley, some other Early Harappan sites like Kot Diji in Sindh or Harappa in Panjab were also fortified, establishing the fact that fortifying the settlements was not a novelty introduced by the Mature Harappans.)

Making a rough parallelogram on plan, the Early Harappan fortification-walls were oriented approximately along the cardinal directions (Fig. 3.3). These enclosed an area measuring about 250 metres north-south and 170 metres east-west. How many gateways there were in all could not be determined since the entire length of these walls was not continuously exposed. However, at the north-west corner a gateway was duly identified, which presented an interesting feature. Here the northern wall turned south-westwards and the western wall first eastwards and then a bit to the north-east, to produce a gateway. The result of such a layout was that the gateway was protected by the curved-in parts of the walls in case of any unauthorized entry or attack. This part was particularly vulnerable since it was located very close to the river-bank. However, this very gate seems to have been used for bringing in material by boats from satellite villages located upstream and downstream.

As already stated, not much area of the habitation inside could be

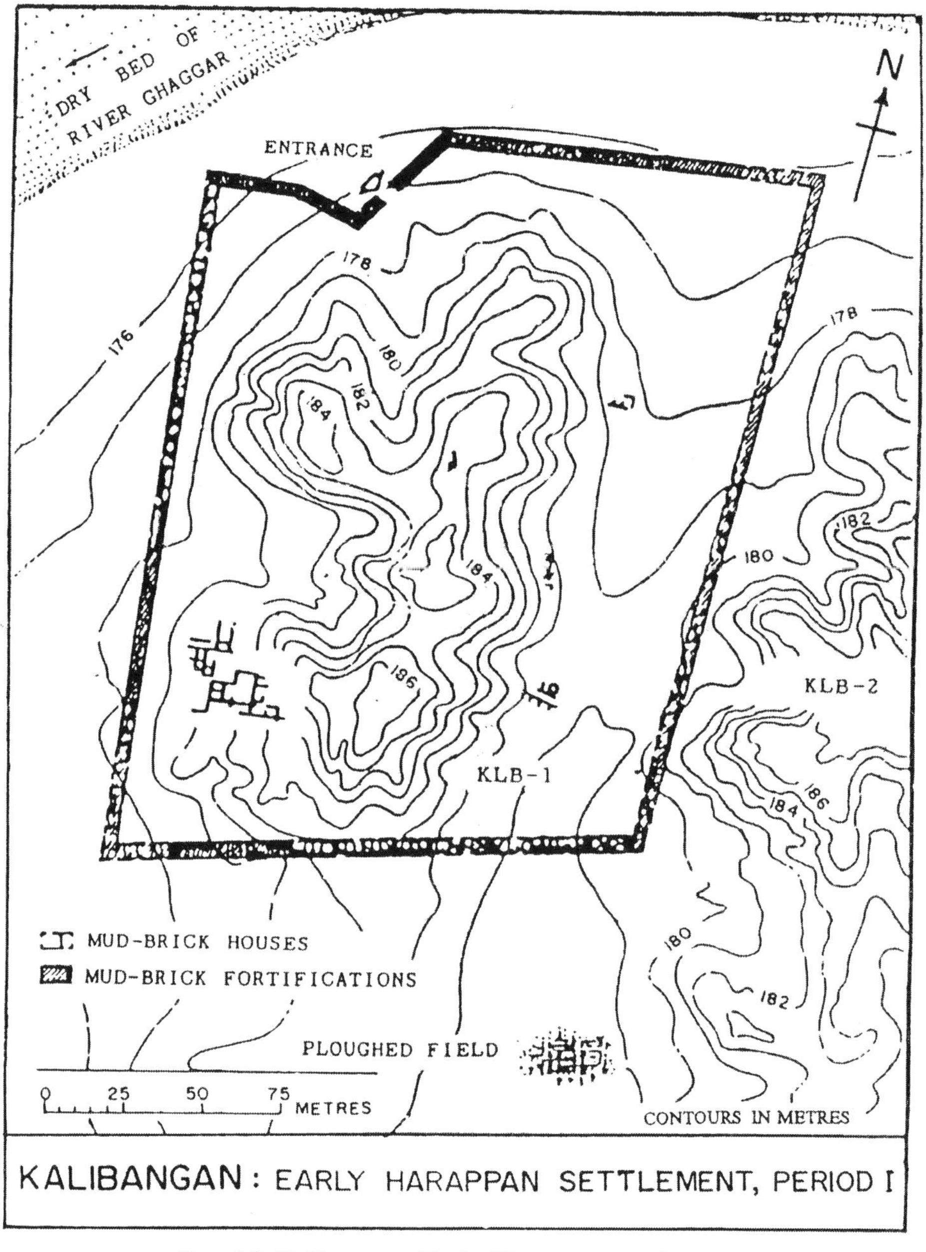

Fig. 3.3 Kalibangan: Early Harappan settlement

Fig. 3.4 Kalibangan: Lane with adjacent houses. Early Harappan

excavated. However, it was duly observed that the houses were also oriented along the cardinal directions. At one place, a lane, measuring 1.5 m in width was also noted running east-west (Fig. 3.4). The usual pattern of a house comprised a courtyard with living rooms around it — a style continued to be followed by the Mature Harappans. Noteworthy, however, was the presence of overground and underground cooking ovens (*tandūrs*) in the courtyard. (More will be said about these *tandūrs* in a subsequent chapter, pp.95-96.) Except in the case of drains wherein kiln-fired bricks were used, mud-bricks were normal in the constructions. Interesting, however, is the fact that in the walls one could see the use of what is known as the 'English bond'. In this method, there are alternate courses of headers and stretchers. Within a total vertical deposit of

Fig. 3.5 Kalibangan: Early Harappan structures

1.6 m, as many as five structural phases were noticed (Fig. 3.5).

Since only a limited area of the Early Harappan times was excavated, not many antiquities could be recovered. However, mention must be made of a variety of copper/bronze objects including bangles, antimony rods, fish-hooks, an axe and a *paraśu*. This last-named tool, it may be added, is still used in Rajasthan for cutting scrubby brushes for firewood. The other antiquities included beads of agate, carnelian, shell, etc.

The Early Harappan pottery of Kalibangan has been divided into six categories on the basis of the fabric. While it is not considered necessary to go into the details of all these, something still needs to be mentioned. The application of a coating of sand-cum-clay on the exterior of some pots and of the occurrence of groups of incised designs on certain other pots remind

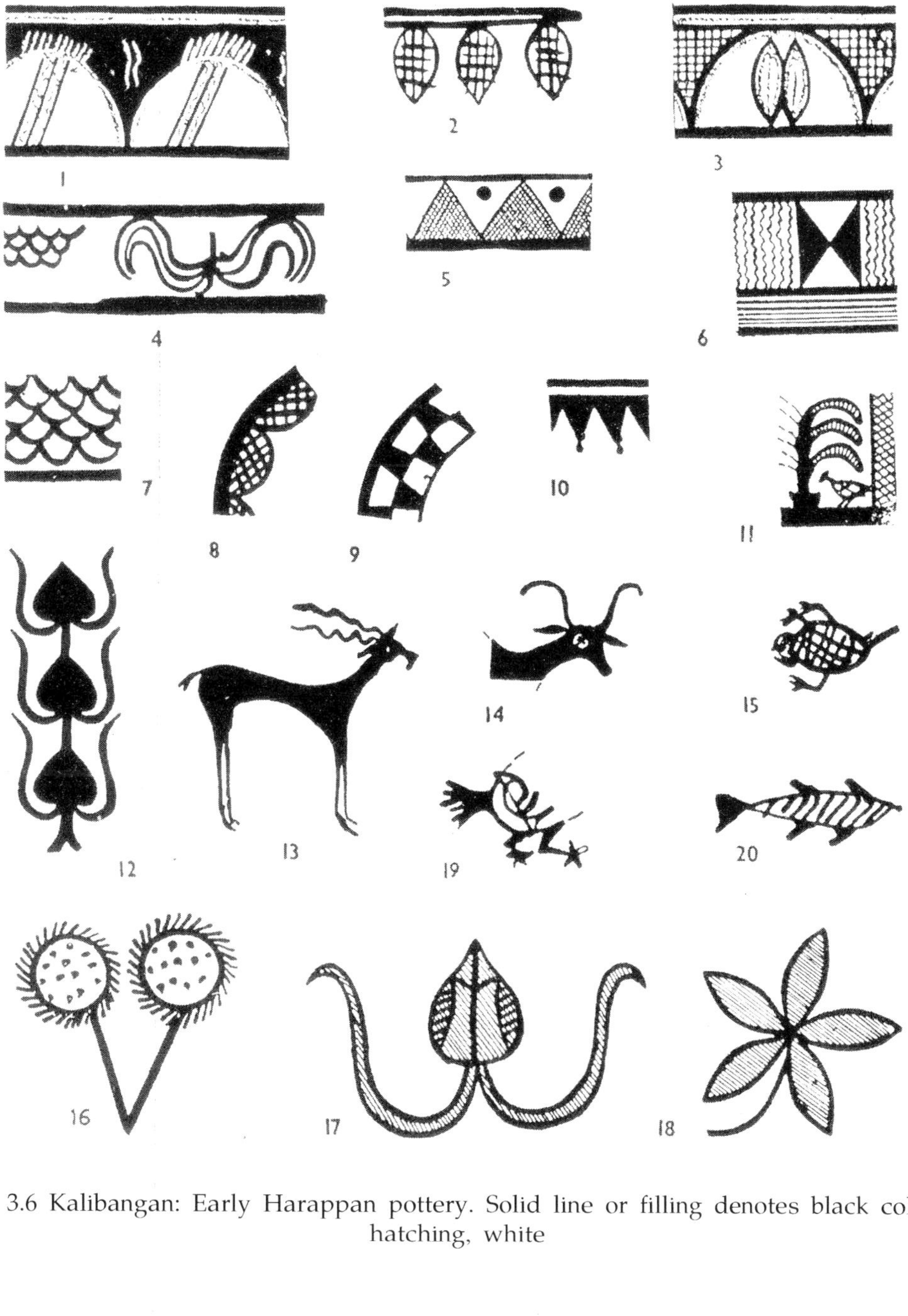

Fig. 3.6 Kalibangan: Early Harappan pottery. Solid line or filling denotes black colour; hatching, white

Fig. 3.7 Kalibangan: Faulted strata, resulting from an earthquake which brought about the end of the Early Harappan settlement

one of a more or less similar treatment of some of the pottery in the Hakra Ware of Cholistan. The use of two colours in painted designs — black outline and white in-filling (Figs. 3.1 and 3.6), as stated earlier, is a feature which Kalibangan shares with all other Early Harappan sites in the Sarasvatī valley and elsewhere. Finally, reference must be made to a fine-grained and well-fired red ware, sometimes slipped and painted with designs mostly in black colour. Not only the fabric but also some of the shapes in it take it nearer to the typical sturdy red ware of the Mature Harappan times.

A remarkable discovery relating to the Early Harappan times at Kalibangan was that of a ploughed agricultural field, with criss-cross furrow-marks oriented north-south and east-west (Figs. 4.31-32). This is the earliest (ca. 2800 BC) agricultural field ever brought to light through an excavation anywhere in the world (Lal 1970-71). Further details of this field, in particular the interesting point about the continuity of this pattern of the furrow-marks up to the modern times, will be discussed later (below, pp.98-101).

This flourishing Early Harappan settlement at Kalibangan was cruelly brought to a sudden end by an earthquake, which left its marks all over. Fig. 3.7 shows a part of this tell-tale story. In the upper portion of this photograph

Fig. 3.8 Kalibangan: Faulted walls of the Early Harappan Period, resulting from an earthquake

one notices a series of layers of which the black ones, because of their colour, are easily identifiable. If only one cares to follow the fate of the uppermost black layer, one would observe that it is ruptured and sinks three to four times. Though not equally clear in the photograph, one may also note the obliquely running cleavage-lines adjacent to the ruptured black horizontal layers. All this points to the violent shaking that the area had undergone. This story is fully corroborated by another photograph reproduced here (Fig. 3.8). In the middle part on the extreme left, one sees not only the rupturing of the layers (mark in particular the black ones) but also the cleavage and subsequent sinking of the walls. This calamity occurred around 2700 BC, as indicated by the radiocarbon dates. Incidentally, this is the earliest earthquake ever identified in an archaeological excavation (Lal 1984).

We now pass on to another site in the Sarasvatī valley, namely Banawali, which shows some further evolutionary trends towards the Mature Harappan stage. From Kalibangan it is at a distance of about 120 km north-east, as the crow flies. The district is Hissar, in Haryana. Covering an area of about 400 x 400 m, the mound rises to a height of about 10 m above the surrounding ground-level (cf. Fig. 3.21). Within this thickness, three cultural periods were identified, viz. Early, Mature and Late Harappan. Right now we are concerned with the Early Harappan, which accounted for a deposit of about 3 m — much thicker than that encountered at Kalibangan but matching that at Kunal. However, since the beginning and end of Banawali seem to be later than those of Kunal, the former site has something more to offer in the evolutionary process.

The excavator (Bisht 1982, 1987; and *Indian Archaeology — A Review 1986-87;* and *1987-88*) has further made out three Sub-periods within the Early Harappan, naming them IA, IB and IC. The point to be noted is that whereas there was no fortification-wall around the settlement during Sub-period IA, it came up in Sub-period IB. It had a basal width of 3.6 m and at one place is available to a height of about 2 m. Sub-period IC revealed something still more interesting. As the excavator puts it (*IAR 1986-87*: 33), this Sub-period is marked by 'drastic and diagnostic changes in architecture, planning and antiquities in an otherwise continuing cultural *milieu* of the preceding sub-period. The entire settlement was planned and constructed *de novo*. The dichotomous layout which the [Mature] Harappans adopted was introduced during this sub-period. The fortification of the previous [sub-]period was externally chiselled or partially sliced away and doubled in width for housing the citadel, and the lower town was laid out contiguously towards the east as well as north, while the position in the west remained unresolved.' It would thus be seen that even the Mature Harappan concept of town-planning, viz. a Citadel and Lower Town, had begun to emerge towards the end of the Early Harappan stage.

As at Kalibangan, so also at Banawali the houses were oriented along the cardinal directions. In the earlier levels, the bricks had the Kalibangan ratio of 3: 2: 1, but soon came into vogue the ratio of 4: 2: 1, which was already there at Kunal, hardly 20 km away. However, Banawali outstripped both these sites in the use of kiln-fired bricks. Thus, while at Kalibangan these were used only to a limited extent, viz. for drains where water was involved, at Banawali their use for the construction of the walls is duly attested to.

In terms of ceramics, whereas the typical Early Harappan bichrome pottery was there, also to be noted was a slipped red ware with some of the Mature Harappan forms. The other antiquities included copper fish-hooks and arrow-heads, beads of carnelian, agate and lapis lazuli and bangles of faience, shell and clay. From the evolutionary angle, however, more noteworthy were

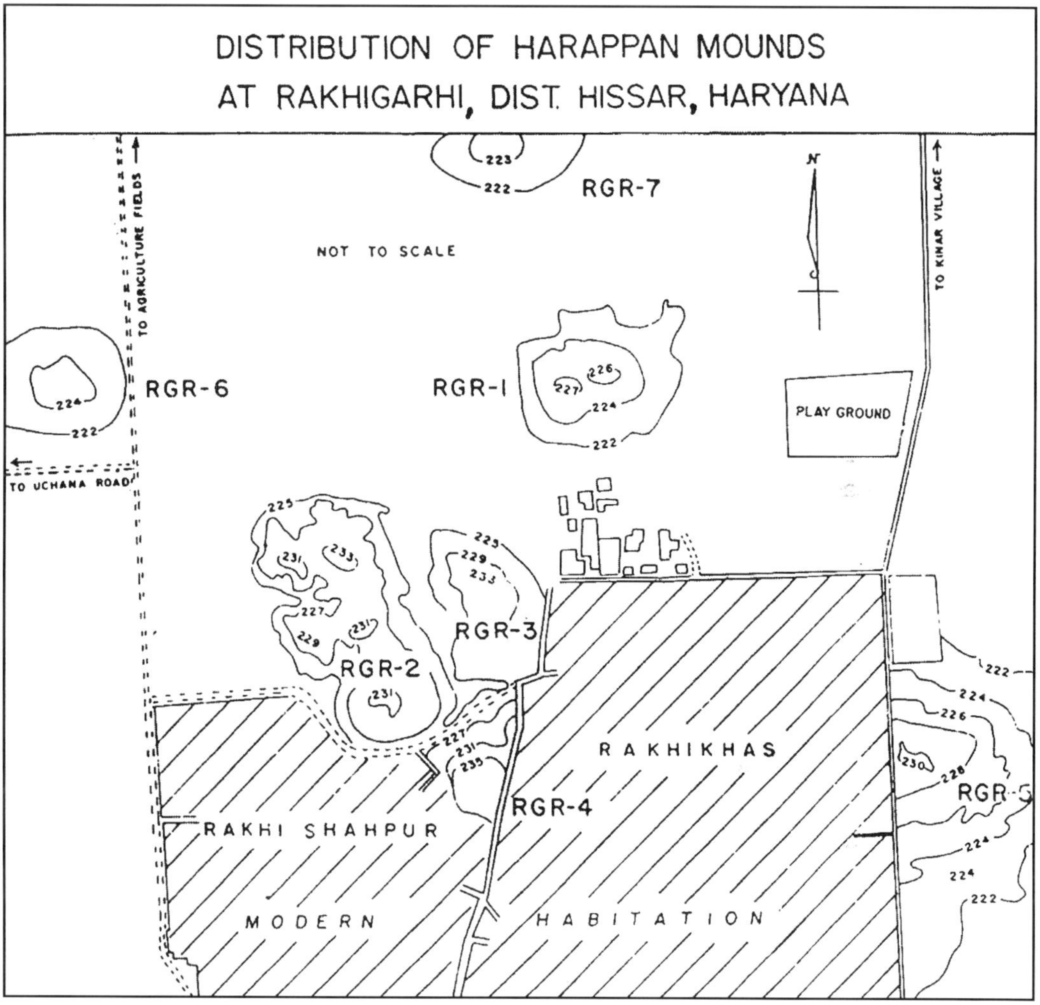

Fig. 3.9 Rakhigarhi: General plan of the site

the terracotta cakes and chert blades. Bisht (1982: 116) also speaks of a weight from the Early Harappan levels: ' ...a stone weight, perhaps the first of its kind. Its weight is 87.855 grams. Although it does not fit into the binary system of Indus weights, it closely approximates a sum a hundred times the supposed unit weight of 0.857 grams, (Marshall 1931: 590-91; Mackay 1938: 602, 606, Table III)'.

Located on the right bank of the ancient Dṛiṣadvatī, which is now known as the Chautang and is for the most part dry, Rakhigarhi can easily claim to have been one of the most flourishing and sizeable cities of the Harappan Civilization, covering an overall area of 105 hectares (Nath 1997-78: 40). Due to erosion over the past several millennia, the peripheral areas of the site have been denuded, but some parts even now stand to a height of 14 m above the surrounding plains. However, it has been further observed that in certain areas the ancient remains go down by another 4.5 m below the plains. Of the ancient mounds, two are somewhat separate, marked RGR-1 and RGR-6 on the plan (Fig. 3.9), while the remaining ones, viz. RGR-2, RGR-3, RGR-4 and RGR-5 are almost contiguous, there being only modern roads in between. In fact, there is no real separation between RGR-4 and RGR-5, since the modern road passes over the top of the mound itself.

Excavations have been carried out at the site during the field-seasons of 1997-98, 1998-99 and 1999-2000 and two short papers have been published by the excavator, Amarendra Nath (1997-98 and 1998-99), briefly outlining the results. However, what is contained in the following pages about Rakhigarhi is based partly on these papers and the information given by the excavator to the present author during the latter's visit to the site and partly on the observations made by the latter himself. As per the evidence obtained so far, RGR-6 seems have been occupied only during the Early Harappan times, whereas the occupation at RGR-1 commenced during the Early Harappan times and continued well into the Mature Harappan days. RGR-3 has not been touched at all because of the presence of a medieval grave on its top, which is under worship and maintained by the local Wakf Board. The southern part of RGR-2 has yielded so far only Mature Harappan structures, though there are indications of Early Harappan remains on its western side. RGR-4 and RGR-5 too have not yielded any Early Harappan remains so far. Although this is not the place to deal with the Late Harappan period, the reader may perhaps be anxious to know whether or not the site continued up to that stage. The answer, based on the evidence available so far, is in the negative. In summary, thus, Rakhigarhi began with a small, though really not so small, settlement during the Early Harappan times, but expanded considerably during the Mature Harappan period. However, it was during the Mature Harappan stage itself that the site was abandoned. The significance of this last observation will be discussed in some detail later.

As already stated, there is no Mature Harappan over-load in RGR-6. Thus, the area is ideally suited for extensive horizontal excavation in order to obtain a good picture of the layout of the Early Harappan times. However, since the land is under intensive cultivation, it has been possible so far to open up only a limited area. Nevertheless, it has been ascertained that the thickness of the Early Harappan deposits over here is more than 4.5 m. Within the top 2.5 m four structural sub-periods have been encountered. Since the area available further down has narrowed because of the above-mentioned structures, it has not been possible to ascertain the number of earlier structural phases, but there are clear floors and ash-cum-charcoal layers to indicate the same. In fact, charcoal samples have been collected from these strata for radiocarbon dating and hopefully the dates will be available in a year or so.

Horizontally, even within this limited area, the remains of three houses have been met with, separated from one another by narrow lanes, which in one case measured only 90 cm in width, but in the other 1.8 m. Whether the former was really a lane used as such or just some space left between the two neighbouring houses it is difficult to say, but surely the latter must have functioned as a lane. In this context, it may be of some interest to note that the width of one of the Mature Harappan lanes at Kalibangan was also 1.8 m. It needs to be added that the houses, as usual even for the Early Harappan stage, were oriented along the cardinal directions.

Of the earliest complex (met with so far), parts of only two structures have been exposed. One has two walls joining each other at right angles and would clearly form a living room, either square or rectangular on plan when fully exposed. The other is circular, with a diameter of 1.90 m. It has also a small opening, 90 cm in width. It is likely that it may have been used for storage, though its use for other purposes cannot be ruled out.

Of the three houses met with in the upper levels, the one on the eastern side has a big courtyard, with rooms on two sides, as exposed so far. In one of the rooms has been noted a circular oven (*tandūr*) having a diameter of 85 cm. It is internally plastered and the side walls and bottom are all red because of long contact with fire. It may be recalled that similar *tandūrs* were met with at Kalibangan. All the houses were made of mud bricks, the size being 36 x 24 x 12 cm or 42 x 28 x 14 cm, which seems to be the standard length: breadth: thickness ratio, viz. 3: 2: 1, in the Early Harappan levels in the

Sarasvatī basin prior to the emergence of 4: 2: 1 ratio towards the end of the Early Harappan, as in Banawali IC.

In the Early Harappan levels in RGR-1 also a circular structure, incidentally having the same internal diameter of 1.9m as in RGR-6, has been noted. This too has an opening, 80 cm in width. However, in this case, the area fronting it is paved with kiln-fired bricks, though broken. If the circular structure was used for storage of grains (though no specimens have been recovered so far), it is not unlikely that the area in front of it may have been used for thrashing the same. A little away from it, to the north, there is a rectangular structure, containing ash, charcoal and pottery. If a guess is to be hazarded, could it have been a kiln?

In the southern part of RGR-1 two houses, oriented along the cardinal directions, have been identified, with a street in between. Through the street there flowed a 75-cm wide drain, made of kiln-fired bricks. Into it there also discharged a drain from the western of the two houses. Though the walls of the houses were made generally of mud bricks, kiln-fired bricks were also used sometimes. However, these latter bricks did not conform to the standard Early Harappan measurements. Incidentally, these also bore curved 'finger'-lines in groups, made evidently before firing — a feature we come across on the bricks even in later times. In one of the rooms of the house on the eastern side there lay two pots side by side, with ash in them. Close by to the east there was a floor paved with brickbats, and a little beyond there were two shallow pits. What kind of activity this complex was associated with it is difficult to say. Maybe, some minor industry? The excavator is of the view that the dyeing of textiles may have been done in this area (Nath 1998-99: 47), though no dyeing material has yet been identified. 'The deposit of ash and shell debitage in the public drain [referred to above] suggested the existence of shell working in the vicinity' (Nath op.cit.).

The pottery found in the Early Harappan levels of Rakhigarhi was similar to that met with at Kalibangan and Banawali. There was the use of two colours — black as well as white — in the painted designs, the former generally used for the outlines and the latter for in-filling. On the exterior of some of the vases there occurred groups of incised wavy lines. In the case of large basins, the incised lines were on the interior, and much thicker. There were also a few grey ware and burnished black ware pots. Mention must also be made of pots on whose exterior there was a 'coating of mud mixed with coarse particles'.

The small finds from the Early Harappan levels included: beads of faience, steatite and semi-precious stones; bangles, needles and arrow-heads of copper/ bronze (metal yet to be analyzed); terracotta bangles, animal figurines and frames of cart-models; and a fluted core of chert. The last-named specimen is significant since the material is not locally available and would point to long-distance trade.

Dhalewan in district Mansa, Panjab, is yet another site which is likely to throw valuable light on the Early Harappan stage. Although a substantial part of the mound has been cut away by agriculturists, there still remains an area measuring about 300 x 300 m. The excavation has revealed in the trenches concerned a deposit of about 5m, of which the lower 2.5 m contains Early Harappan material, followed by the Mature Harappan. The later strata are associated with Kushan and Gupta times with which we are not concerned here. (Madhu Bala and Vishnu Kant 2000.)

The Early Harappan levels have yielded pottery similar to that found at Kalibangan, Kunal, etc. However, special mention must be made of perforated jars and dishes-on-stand in sturdy red ware, both of which duly anticipate the typical Mature Harappan pottery. The small finds include carnelian and steatite beads, faience bangles, terracotta 'cakes' of all shapes (including the *muṣṭikās*) and, more importantly, a small-sized cubical stone weight. So far four structural sub-periods have been identified, the walls, made of mud bricks, being oriented along the cardinal directions. The size of the bricks falls in the ratio of 3:2:1, the actual measurements being 30 x 20 x 10 or 33 x 22 x 11 or 36 x 24 x 12. Though not yet fully clear, one of the structures appears to have been a fortification wall. **All told, it is becoming increasingly clear that there was a considerable expanse of the Early Harappan culture in the basins of the Sarasvatī and its tributaries and that this cultural complex was heading towards the Mature Harappan.**

(III) AT MATURITY

As seen in the foregoing pages, the way to the Mature Harappan stage was already being paved during the Early Harappan times, and this provides full justification for the kind of nomenclature we have given to the two cultural stages. But certain very distinctive elements, such as weights, measures, inscribed seals and sealings, a full-fledged system of writing, elegant statuary and elaborate town-planning with monumental buildings, which are the hall-mark of the Mature stage, had yet to appear in their fullness. For example, so far only a few examples of weights have been reported from the Early Harappan assemblages, viz. at Harappa and Banawali. Or, barring one example from Harappa (information from Richard Meadow) or another from Rehman Dheri, the Early Harappan seals do not bear the typical inscription and animal motif, though shape-wise these may be similar to those from the Mature stage (for example at Kunal). Likewise, while we do have graffiti on the pottery from the Early Harappan levels, many of which are similar to the signs of the Mature Harappan script, regular inscriptions, but for an odd example here or there, are wanting. The question then is: How did this all-round 'revolution' take place within a slow yet steady 'evolution' ? While a clear-cut answer is difficult to offer, something in that direction may nevertheless be stated.

It would be readily agreed to that out of the above-mentioned differentiating list, the first four, viz. weights, measures, seals and writing, evidently pertain to trade and commerce. The weights and measures must have been produced in order to weigh and measure the commodities that were exported/imported. That the seals were actually used for sealing packages containing such commodities is fully borne out by the occurrence of as many as 65 clay sealings in the ruins of a warehouse at Lothal, which had accidentally caught fire. The sealings were also affected by the fire. However, these bear on one side marks left by the reeds/cloth and thread used in packaging and on the other impressions of the seals. Added to the foregoing is the fact that this warehouse was located in the vicinity of the dockyard which was visited by boats coming from the Gulf of Khambhat. All this duly testifies to the seaborne trade that the Mature Harappan Civilization was having via the Arabian Sea. And the destination was the entire region comprising the eastern part of the Arabian peninsula, islands in the Persian Gulf and southern Iraq. A great deal of material of Indian origin has been found at excavated sites in these regions. A more important point to note is that, based on West Asian evidence, this contact dates back to a time around 2600 BC. Ascribable to about the same time, overland trade also flourished with north-eastern Iran and parts of Central Asia. And this indeed is the time when the aforesaid 'revolution' from the Early to Mature Harappan stage did take place, as indicated by the radiocarbon dates for the early levels of the Mature Harappan stage at Indian sites (Lal 1997: 252-53). The invention of a full-fledged system of writing also seems to fall in line with a sharp augmentation in trade, since records had to be maintained of the incoming and outgoing commodities and of the manner in which the financial transactions were made. Spurt in trade must have given rise to tremendous affluence. And this in turn must have brought about a qualitative change in the style of living — in housing, elaborate layout of the settlements, improved civic amenities like an underground drainage system, and the coming up of monumental buildings such as large-sized granaries, assembly halls, ritualistic platforms, ceremonial baths and so on. The elites must have also thought in terms of decorating their houses with statues, both in metal and stone, and the ladies must have vied with one another in bedecking themselves, resulting in the production of fine jewellery. And this is where the Mature Harappan Civilization stands out from its mother — the Early Harappan.

In the preceding paragraphs we have referred to a kind of 'revolution' which provided the quantum jump from the slow yet steady 'evolution' that was already taking place during the Early Harappan times. One might now pose another question, namely where exactly did this revolution take place within the vast area over which the Early Harappan remains have been encountered — from Rehman Dheri in the north-west to Kot Diji in the south-west to Kunal in the north-east? While a categorical answer is evidently difficult to arrive at, an attempt to look for it can nevertheless be made.

Although there exists a large Mature Harappan site, viz. Dabar Kot, in the hilly tracts west of the Indus, it is doubtful if this region could have provided the necessary environmental and ecological setting for the growth of a riverine civilization that the Mature Harappan was. A couple of such sites may have come up in this hilly region as intermediary stations in the context of overland trade between the main-region Mature Harappan sites on the one hand and Afghanistan, north-east Iran and Central Asia on the other.

Within the plains, from the Indus on the west and Yamunā on the east, the following facts and figures seem to speak for themselves. Misra (1994: 512-13) has given a very good summary of the available data. Accordingly, in the valleys of the Indus and of its main tributaries, viz. the Jhelum, Chenab and Ravi, right from the Panjab down to Sindh, Misra has noted a total of 50

Harappan sites (both Early and Mature) — 44 in Sindh and only six in Panjab (Pakistan). In marked contrast, in the valleys of the Sarasvatī and its former tributaries, which have now either dried up or have changed their course, the number is very much larger. Mughal's survey of the Sarasvati–Hakra valley in Cholistan (Pakistan) brought to light 40 Early Harappan and 174 Mature Harappan sites. Likewise, Joshi and his colleagues recorded 137 Early and 109 Mature Harappan settlements in the valleys of the Sarasvatī and its tributaries in India (Joshi *et al.* 1984). These data tend to suggest that the hub of this 'revolution' may have been the region comprising the Sarasvatī basin and the lower parts of the valleys of the Ravi and the Indus.

Having given some thought to the rise of the Mature stage of the Harappan Civilization and the possible epicentre of the 'revolution', we may now turn our attention to some settlements representing this stage in the region under discussion, namely the Sarasvatī valley.

While Mughal, as stated, has plotted as many as 174 Mature Harappan sites in the Hakra (ancient Sarasvatī) valley in Cholistan, it is a matter of some regret that not even a single site has been excavated. Spread over an area measuring no less than 81.5 hectares, Ganweriwala is an ideal Mature Harappan site awaiting the spade. Maybe Mughal himself or someone else takes it up in the foreseeable future.

Anyway, we may now pass on to the Sarasvatī valley on the Indian side of the border. Over here many a site has been excavated, but we shall take up only the more noteworthy ones, namely Kalibangan, Banawali and Rakhigarhi.

While dealing with the Early Harappan stage, we already referred to the location and general configuration of the mounds at Kalibangan. To recall briefly, there were two principal mounds, a smaller one (KLB-1) on the west and a larger one (KLB-2) on the east. The former has been called the 'Citadel', while the latter, the 'Lower Town'. Though this bipartite arrangement of the settlement was duly known both from Mohenjo-daro and Harappa, it has to be noted that it was for the first time at Kalibangan that both these parts were found to have been fortified (Fig. 3.10).

The 'Citadel' at Kalibangan was sited over the ruins of the Early Harappan times, perhaps to give to it a 'higher' position vis-a-vis the 'Lower Town' which came up on the adjacent natural soil. In fact, for quite some length on the

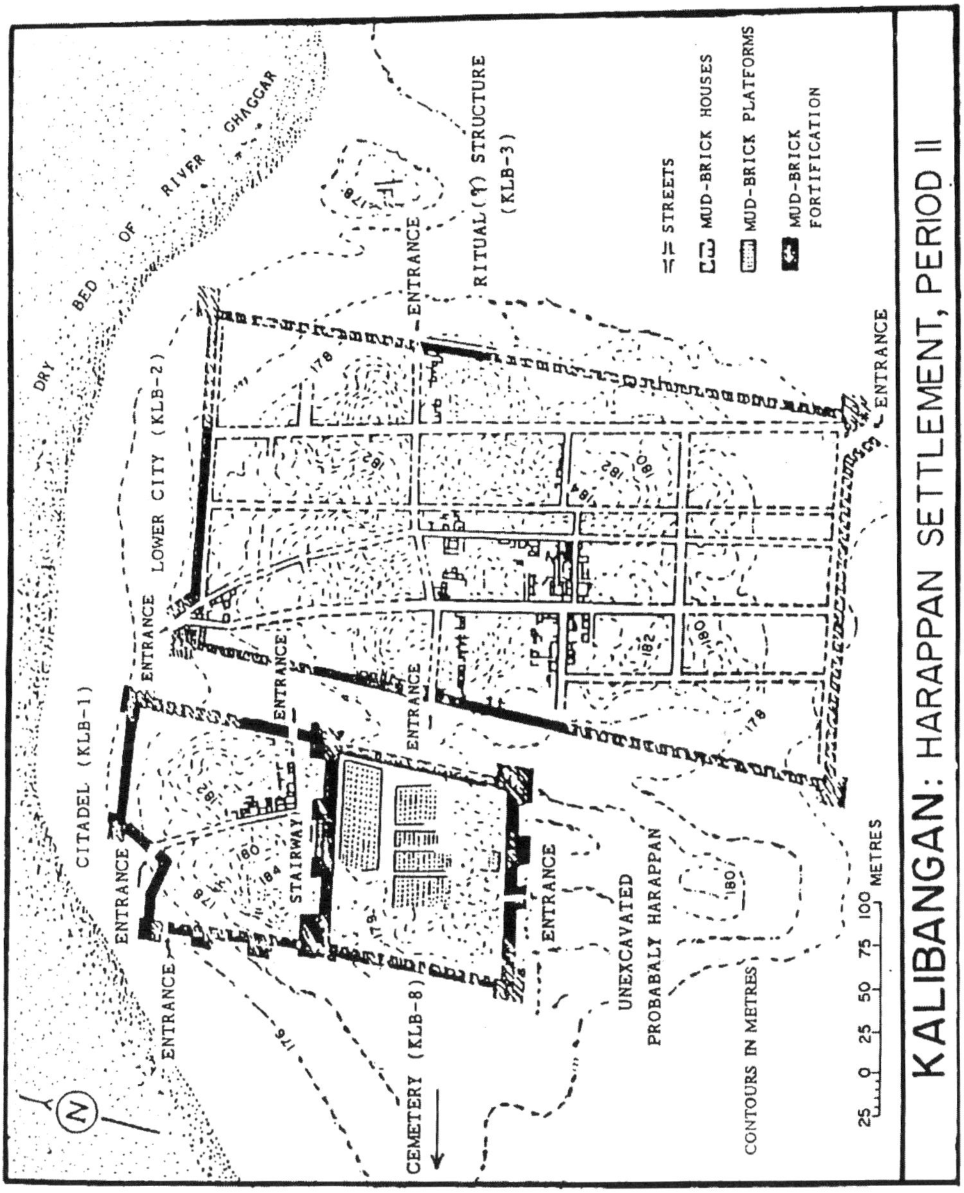

Fig. 3.10 Kalibangan: Harappan settlement, Period II

western as well as northern sides the Mature Harappan fortification-walls were built utilizing the extant height of the Early Harappan ones. On the southern side, however, the Mature Harappans made some adjustments, while on the eastern they laid out a fresh wall. All this was done to keep the overall dimensions of the Citadel in a set ratio of 2:1, the north-south length being 240 m and the east-west 120 m. The orientation, as usual, was along the cardinal directions.

The Citadel was further divided into two equal parts, by laying out a medial east-west wall. It is also interesting to note that the structures that were put up in these two parts were of different nature, though put together they responded to an integrated scheme. In the southern part there were a series of mud-brick platforms, each separated from the other by an intermediary passage. There was also a passage between these platforms and the fortification-walls. Although the upper levels of most of these platforms had been denuded by the ravages of nature and man over the millennia, at least in two cases it was possible to make out their purpose. In one case there stood a brick-lined pit containing bovine bones and antlers, indicative of animal-sacrifice (see Fig. 4.58, p.121). Over the other platform were identified seven contiguous 'fire-altars' (see Fig. 4.60, p.122), with a well and bathing pavement close by. While more will be said about these remains in a subsequent chapter (pp.119-23), it is pretty clear that these had ritualistic associations. Quite in consonance with this aspect, one finds the nature of the entrances to this southern part. There were two of these, one through the medial wall, which allowed entry from the northern part and the other through the southern fortification-wall. In both cases there was provision of steps, with the result that no vehicular traffic could enter this part. Persons could only walk into it, and circumambulate the religious structures, if they so wished. Evidently riding around religious buildings was not considered to be in good taste.

As against the foregoing, the entrances to the northern part were in level with the ground and vehicles could freely get in and out. Of these, one was located opposite the Lower Town so as to let in the residents from that area. The other was in the north-west corner close to the river and was evidently meant to facilitate movement of men and material via the river. However, a more important point to be noted is that in this part of the Citadel there were no ritualistic platforms. There were only residential buildings on both sides of a street that, starting from near the partition-wall, approached the north-

Fig. 3.11 Kalibangan: Brick-on-edge pathway, running along the northern side of the partition-wall of the Citadel. Mature Harappan

west gate. Interesting also is the fact that the street emerging from the eastern gate and passing between the houses and the partition-wall was paved with mud bricks (Fig. 3.11). It terminated near the stepped entrance leading from the northern part into the southern. It appears that the residential houses in the northern part were occupied by priests who conducted/supervised the rituals performed on the platforms in the southern part. If one is permitted to let imagination run, it would seem that the paved pathway was a ceremonial one on which marched a procession of the priests while entering the southern part to conduct the rituals.

Some 40 m to the east of the Citadel was the Lower Town. As already stated, this too was fortified. While the eastern and western fortification-walls faithfully followed the cardinal directions, that on the northern side showed

Fig. 3.12 Kalibangan: The widest (7.2 m) street in the Lower Town. Mature Harappan

a slight deviation. The southern part of the mound having undergone heavy erosion, over here the fortification-wall could not be located. However, it may justifiably be assumed that originally it did exist and that it ran parallel to the one on the north. While the width of the Lower Town was noted to be 240 m, its exact north-south length would remain conjectural, because of the non-detection of the southern fortification-wall. However, on the basis of the extant habitation-debris on this side, the length may well have been around 360 m. Mud bricks were used in the construction of the fortifications. Initially, these were of a larger size, measuring 40 x 20 x 10 cm, but later on bricks of the same size as used for the construction of the houses inside, viz. 30 x 15 x 7.5 cm were used. Kiln-fired bricks were also sometimes used in the fortifications,

Fig. 3.13 Kalibangan: Another street in the Lower Town. Mature Harappan

but only for a limited purpose.

Four major streets, running all the way north-south, were duly identified (Fig. 3.10). Also noted was a street of lesser length in the south-western part. It is likely that there may have also existed a similar short street in the north-east. Two of these major streets joined each other at the north-western corner where there was a gateway, opening out on the river-front. Like the north-south streets, not all the east-west streets ran right across the town. Some of them were staggered. One of these streets approached a gateway on the west, which led to the Citadel. A very interesting feature was noted in respect of the width of these streets. It was in the ratio of 1:2:3:4, the respective widths actually being 1.8 m (evidently a lane), 3.6 m, 5.4 m and 7.2 m (Figs. 3.12-13). It must also go to the credit of the civic authorities at Kalibangan that,

Fig. 3.14 Kalibangan : A drain discharging into a soakage jar embedded in the street immediately outside the house. Mature Harappan

although there were nine structural phases, one following the other, at no point of time was there any encroachment on the streets. The small platforms (*chabūtarās*) abutting the sides of the doorways were, of course, a recognized part of the house-plan.

The houses usually comprised a large courtyard around which, on three sides, were the living rooms, while facing the street was the entrance. The rooms were often paved with mud-bricks, but in one case — perhaps the residence of a very rich person — kiln-fired tiles with decoration of intersecting circles were used. In the courtyard there was an elongated plinth with depressions at the top in some of which was placed fodder and in others the lower halves of pots, filled with water, all meant for the cattle. Some of the houses also had a well of their own (see Fig. 4.38, p.103). Though the Kalibanganites did not construct underground drains, fairly good arrangement was made for the disposal of sullage. The drains discharged into large pots juxtaposed to the exterior wall of the house (Fig. 3.14) and arrangements were made to clear the sullage regularly.

The people on the whole were well-to-do, as indicated not only by their houses but also by the objects left behind. Amongst the more noteworthy ones, attention may be drawn to two figurines of bull, one in terracotta (Fig. 3.15) and the other in bronze (Fig. 3.16). These are full of vigour and vivacity and demonstrate the artistic acumen of the respective craftsmen. There were many examples of the superbly carved steatite seals, but a cylindrical one is particularly remarkable (Fig. 3.17), not only for the intriguing scene it depicts but also for the fact that cylindrical seals are not normal to the Harappan Civilization and thus point to West Asian contact/influence. Attesting to such a contact, once again, is a terracotta *kernos* which consists of a hollow ring with seven lamps attached to its upper surface (Fig. 3.18). From its history in the west, it seems to have been filled with oil, the lamps lighted and the piece carried on the head during religious processions.

Now to the funerary practices of these inhabitants of the Sarasvatī valley. As revealed by the excavations at Harappa, the normal way of disposing the dead body was to intern it in a rectangular pit, in a supine posture, with the head to the north. In the grave were also placed goods like pottery, objects of toiletry, some foodstuff, perhaps under the belief that these might be of use to the departed one in the other world. At Kalibangan quite a few examples of this kind of burial were encountered. In one case, however, the large-sized pit was lined with a wall of mud-bricks, which was also plastered (Fig. 3.19). The number of pots placed was also very large — thirty-seven to the north of the head and 35 below the body. Evidently, the person buried was someone special.

In addition to the aforesaid mode, Kalibangan offered some further evidence which is at once interesting yet intriguing. Within the cemetery area there were grave-pits of the same shape and dimensions as those in the regular graves referred to above. But these were bereft of the body — complete or even partial. Nevertheless, the grave goods were there: pottery and even bangles and beads. And what is more intriguing is that in each of the pits of this category there were a series of layers of sand and clay. Is it that the dead body was first placed in these pits and after the performance of certain rituals it was taken to the regular graves and buried there for ever? Such a hypothesis will, however, remain in the realm of conjecture.

This takes us to another conjecture. In the same general cemetery area,

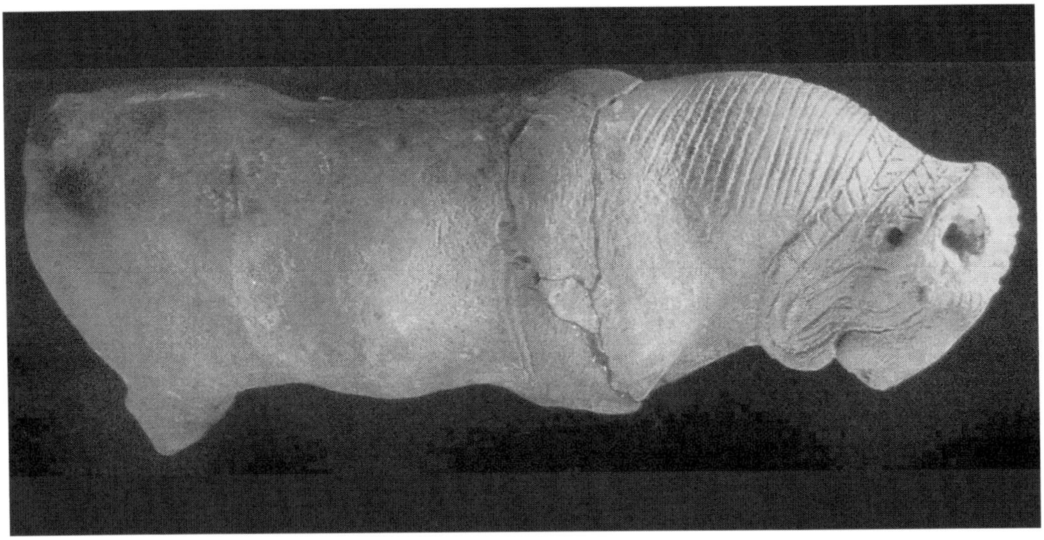

Fig. 3.15 Kalibangan: Terracotta bull. Mature Harappan

Fig. 3.16 Kalibangan: Bronze bull. Mature Harappan

Fig. 3.17 Kalibangan: Cylinder seal and its impression. Mature Harappan

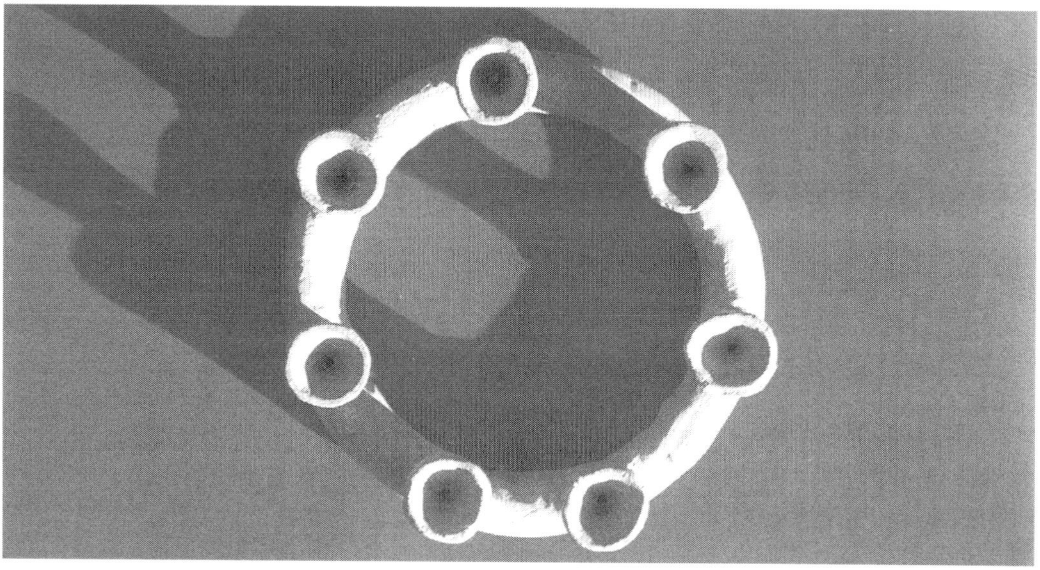

Fig. 3.18 Kalibangan: Terracotta *kernos*. Mature Harappan

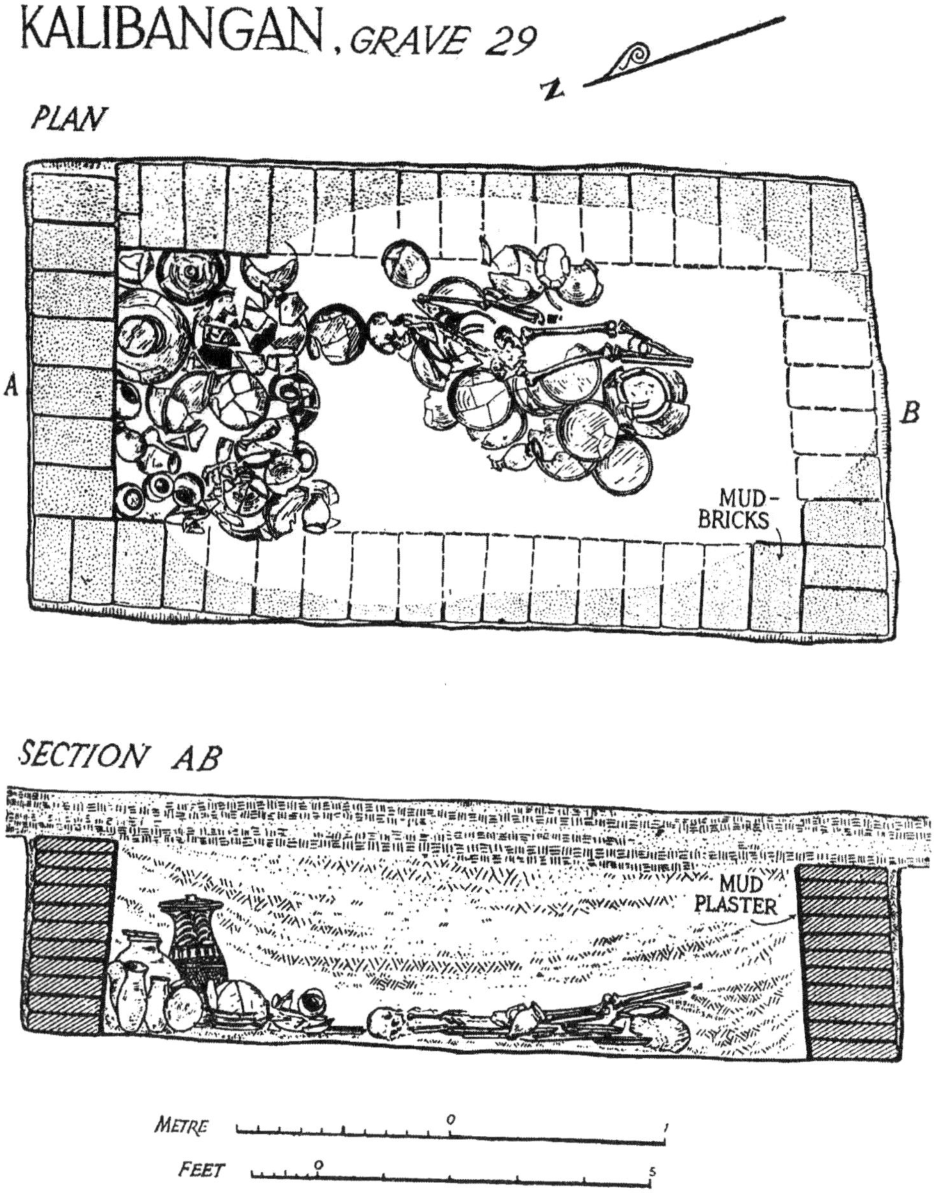

Fig. 3.19 Kalibangan: Grave 29. Mature Harappan

Fig. 3.20 Kalibangan: Burial in a circular pit, with pottery, bronze mirror, etc., but without skeletal remains. Mature Harappan

but a little away from the aforesaid two types, there were circular — not oblong — pits. These also contained a lot of pottery and other funerary goods, including a mirror in one case (Fig. 3.20). But, again, there were no skeletal remains, except for a fragmentary bone in one case. Amidst the plethora of pottery, there always was a large globular jar, standing out from the rest. It was thought, during the course of excavations, that this might contain ashes and charred bones of the departed, after his/her cremation. But nothing like this turned up. Do then these circular examples represent symbolic burials for those who had died elsewhere, or even disposed of in the nearby river because of some specific reasons? As already stated, again a conjecture.

We may now proceed to another very important site, viz. Banawali, some 120 km upstream from Kalibangan. A reference has already been made to it in the context of the Early Harappan remains (above, pp.39-41). An important

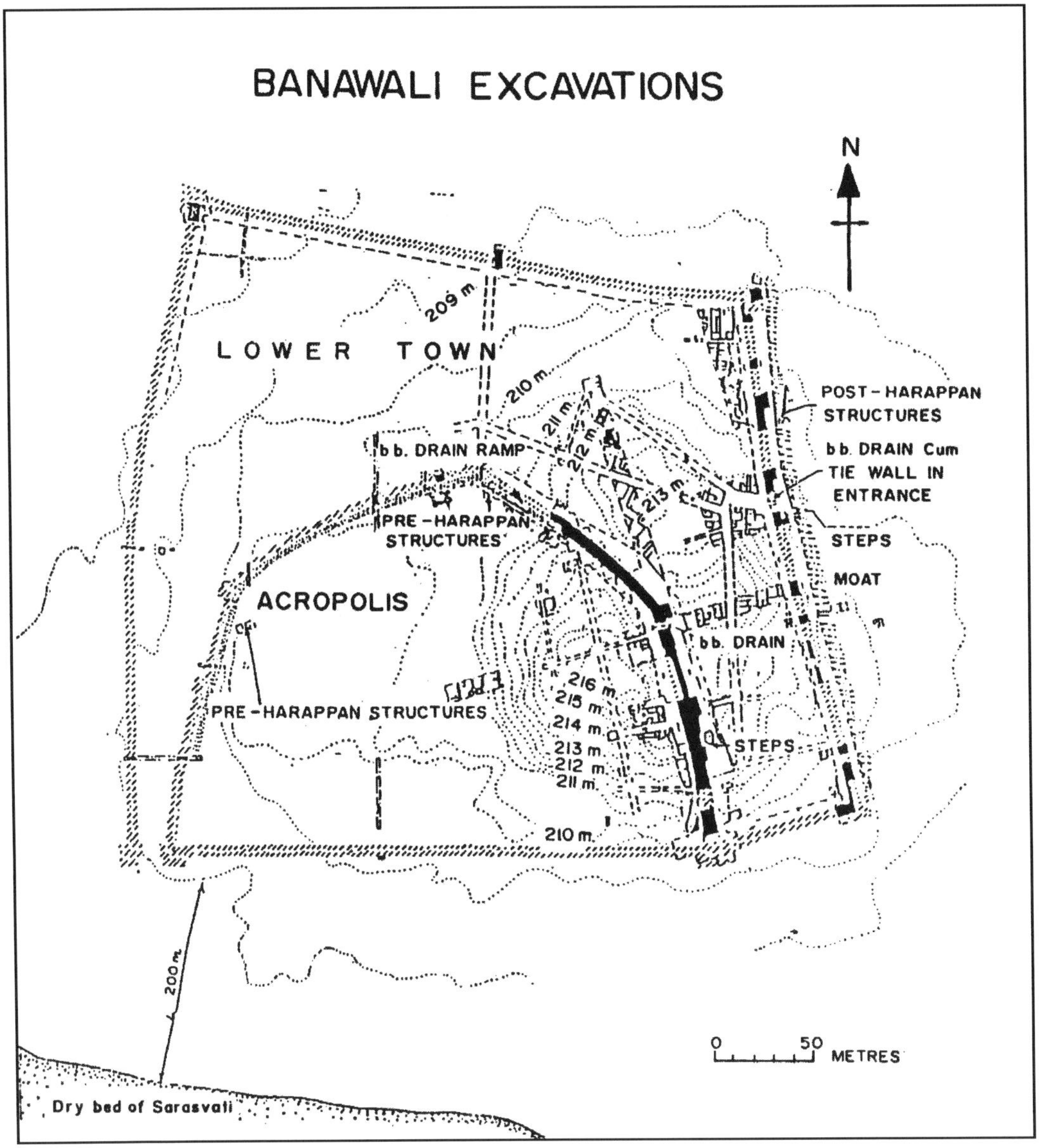

Fig. 3.21 Banawali Excavations

Fig. 3.22 Banawali: Section across the moat. Mature Harappan

point to recall is that at Banawali there was a continuity from the Early stage to the Mature, quite unlike at Kalibangan where there was a break in between. Also, as stated earlier, the concept of a Citadel had already emerged towards the end of the Early Harappan times (Sub-period IC). However, during Period II (Mature Harappan) the layout became elaborate, though not on the lines of Kalibangan. Whereas at the latter site the Citadel and Lower Town were situated separately, with gap of about 40 m, at Banawali these were integrated (Fig. 3.21). Thus, within an overall fortified area, measuring 400 x 400 m, both the Citadel and the Lower Town were sited, there being a common wall for both, on the southern side. Using this common wall, the Citadel formed a sort of semi-ellipse and occupied nearly half of the entire area. The wall fortifying the Citadel had a thickness varying from 5.4 m to 7 m. On the exterior of the eastern side two square bastions were also identified, near one of which there seems to have been a narrow exit. At the apex on the northern side there was a ramp, paved with kiln-fired bricks, which functioned as a passage between the Citadel and the Lower Town. Within the Citadel a few streets were identified, which formed a grid-pattern, running east-west and north-south. It may incidentally be mentioned that no platforms, like those at Kalibangan, were discovered, though it also must be added that only a limited area (a fraction of the eastern part) within the Citadel was excavated.

The streets in the Lower Town did not follow the conventional Mature Harappan gridiron pattern. Instead, from a piazza, facing the entrance through the eastern fortification-wall, the streets shot off in different directions. Thus, from the western end of this piazza there emerged three streets, running respectively in the southern, western and north-western directions. At the eastern end of the piazza and running along the inner face of the aforementioned fortification-wall there was a street which led, in one direction, to north-east corner, and in the other to the south-eastern end. Through chance or by design (?), the width of the wider streets was 5.4 m, reminding us of the wider streets at Kalibangan. On the external side of this fortification-wall there were square bastions. But what is most noteworthy is the provision of a moat (Fig. 3.22). While the moat was duly recorded on the eastern side, one very much wishes that it was also identified on the other sides. Unfortunately, for whatever constraints, this was not done. Nevertheless, the construction of a moat is indeed an addition to our knowledge of the Harappan fortification-system. As regards the supply of water to the moat, there evidently was no problem. The river was already there, whose dry bed may still be seen close on the south (Fig. 3.21). A channel would have been easily taken out from the upstream levels of the river to feed the moat, letting the excess water discharge back into the downstream part of the river. We have a very good example of this kind of arrangement from Śiśupālgarh, a fortified site in Orissa, dating back to the fourth-third century BC, if not earlier (Lal 1949).

The houses followed the usual pattern of having a courtyard with rooms around it. The rooms also were often paved with mud-bricks. A couple of interesting features, however, were noticed at Banawali. In one of the houses, the toilet 'was provided with a wash-basin placed on a high place in a corner near the drain which carried off the waste water into a sullage jar placed outside on the street' (Bisht 1982: 117). The provision of alcoves, within the

Fig. 3.23 Banawali: An apsidal structure associated with 'fire-altars'. Mature Harappan

thickness of the walls, was another noteworthy feature. These measured about 1 m in width and 1 m to 2 m in length. Yet another feature calls for attention. While the presence of 'fire-altars' was something with which we were already familiar from Kalibangan, the evidence from Banawali seems to add another dimension. Over here an apsidal structure was associated with these altars (Fig. 3.23) and some scholars are inclined to think that here is a case for some kind of a 'temple'.

Banawali has yielded a good deal of antiquities, which included a variety of copper objects, beads, bangles, seals, sealings and weights. In this context particular mention may be made of a house wherein, besides a large number of beads, made variously of carnelian, lapis lazuli and gold, there also occurred tiny weights which may have been used for weighing these precious objects. The discovery of a 'touchstone bearing gold streaks of different hues' is rather exciting, since this technique of testing the purity of gold is used even to this day.

We may now turn our attention to Rakhigarhi which is currently under excavation. The location and other topographical details of the site have already been given while dealing with the Early Harappan stage (pp.41-42). In so far as the Mature Harappan period is concerned, it is RGR-2 which has yielded some valuable information. On the western periphery of this mound the remains of a fortification-wall have been duly identified. Made of mud bricks and oriented north-south, it has a basal width of more than 12 m. It has been traced to a length of 30 m and is now available to a height of 3 m. Both the faces, i.e. exterior as well as interior, are sloping, the slope being provided by the setting of successive courses of the bricks a little inwards. This can be seen clearly on the exterior. However, the inner side has a thick coat of mud plaster and hence in the parts so far exposed the actual setting of the courses cannot be seen. The bricks have the standard Mature Harappan ratio of 4: 2: 1. Although deep digging has yet to be done on the inner side of the fortification wall, preliminary indications are that there are pre-fortification deposits in this area, the nature of which is likely to become clear during the next field-season.

The southward continuation of the fortification-wall has also been confirmed in another trench. Over here an additional feature has also been noticed. A construction of kiln-fired bricks seems to suggest a kind of stepped entrance, the details of which are likely to become clear with some more work.

In the southern part of this very mound (RGR-2) have been exposed, though partially, two mud-brick podia, oriented along the cardinal directions. These are provided with a facing of kiln-fired bricks. Atop these podia there lay certain structural features which throw valuable light on the religious practices of the Mature Harappans at Rakhigarhi. These comprised sacrificial pits and 'fire-altars'. There were two sacrificial pits which, oriented along the cardinal directions, measured respectively 3.25 x 1.1x.95 m and 1.75 x 1 x .95 m. These contained bones, horns, hoofs, etc. of cattle and goat. The 'fire-altars', also two in number, were, however, located contiguously. These contained stele as well as terracotta circular 'cakes'. Their orientation was, again, along the cardinal directions and behind them was a north-south wall, indicating that the performers of the ritual had to face the east. It may be recalled that more

Fig. 3.24 Rakhigarhi: A pottery-kiln. Mature Harappan

or less similar sacrificial pits and fire-altars had been found on the podia in the Citadel at Kalibangan. The presence of the fortification wall as well as the podia in RGR-2 would seem to assign a similar status to this part of the settlement at Rakhigarhi.

As stated earlier, the occupation at RGR-1 began during the Early Harappan times and continued well into the Mature stage. While ascribable to the latter there were the usual houses oriented along the cardinal directions, special interest attaches to a complex, laid below the then ground-level and located in a somewhat peripheral part of the mound. On plan, its main body is circular, there being two relatively much smaller semi-circular adjuncts, one each on the western and eastern sides. Thus, it may be said to vaguely resemble a conch (Fig. 3.24). It measures 5 m in the east-west direction and 2.92 m in

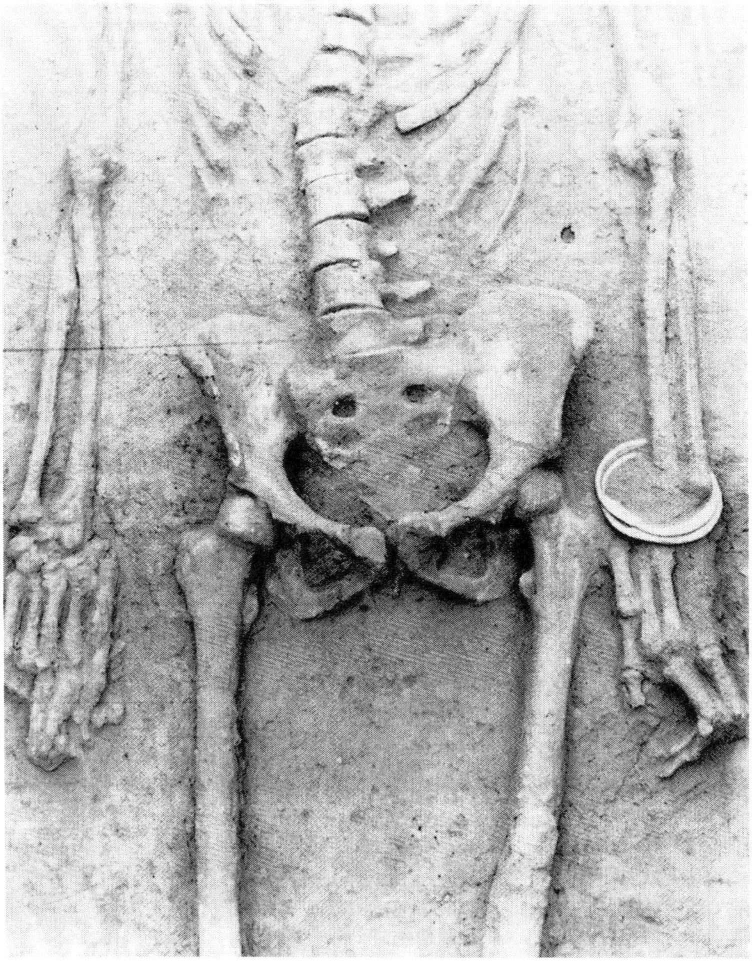

Fig. 3.25 Rakhigarhi: Burial; mark the shell bangles on the left wrist. Mature Harappan

the north-south, and has a depth of 1.30 m. In the middle part there are two independent free-standing shafts, made of kiln-fired bricks. On plan, these have an arch-like curvature, each being 46 cm in width. The side walls of the conch-shaped pit have a thick plaster which is red. And so are the sides and tops of the two free-standing shafts. In the vertical section across the complex, there lay, above the burnt-red bottom, a 30-cm thick deposit of ash and charcoal. This was overlain by a thick debris comprising brick-bats. While it is evident that this pit was associated with some kind of firing activity and may well have been a potter's kiln, no pots as such were met with inside. Maybe after the last use of the kiln, the pots had all been systematically removed. Since the size of the kiln is not very large, it is probable that it was used for firing small to medium-sized vases and not big storage jars. Be that as it may, the overall plan of the kiln is indeed interesting.

The smaller antiquities recovered from the Mature Harappan levels at Rakhigarhi comprised the usual ones — steatite seals, weights, chert blades, copper tools, terracotta figurines. Particular attention may be drawn to a terracotta animal figurine which looks like that of a horse, a plano-convex lead ingot and an elongated sealing with a triangular cross-section. The sealing has inscriptions on two sides and a standing human figure (some deity ?), flanked by horned snakes, on the third.

At a distance of about a hundred metres north of RGR-1 is an area named RGR-7. Over here, a few years ago some human bones had turned up while the villagers were digging a well. Working on this clue, the excavator put up a few trenches and discovered a regular cemetery of the Mature Harappan times. Although about a dozen graves were identified, only seven of them were found intact, the remaining having been disturbed. The disposition of the dead body followed the typical Harappan pattern. It was laid supine, in an extended posture with the head to the north. There was the usual pottery accompaniment. However, it is interesting to note that in one case the dead wore two shell bangles on the left wrist (Fig. 3.25). Although, based on the field-observations, the excavator is inclined to think that the person concerned was a female, a scientific report is still awaited. Anyway, in the case of the cemetery at Harappa, Dales and Kenoyer (1991: 195) state: 'Four burials of what are probably **adult females were found with shell bangles on their left arms**.' Thus, the fact that adult females continued to wear shell bangles even after death becomes an important socio-ritualistic feature amongst the Harappan women. In this context, it would be well worthwhile mentioning that in the eastern parts of India women have to wear shell bangles at the time of their marriage and continue to do so all through their lives, as long as their husband is alive. In case they predecease the husband, I am told, the bangles are retained on the wrists even when they are taken out for cremation.

(IV) THE MYTHS OF 'ARYAN INVASION' AND 'EXTINCTION' OF THE HARAPPAN CIVILIZATION

It is interesting, nay even amusing, to look back and see how historical theories take birth, are sustained and become so much ingrained in the psyche that it becomes next to impossible for conservative scholars even to have a look at the mounting new evidence which goes counter to their long-cherished views. And this is precisely what has happened in the case of the theory known as 'The Aryan Invasion of India'.

In the second half of the nineteenth century, Max Muller, a renowned scholar of Sanskrit, declared that the *Vedas* were no earlier than 1200 BC. This he did on a very ad hoc basis. Granting that the *Sūtra* literature may have existed in the sixth-fifth centuries BC, he assigned a duration of two hundred years to each of the preceding literary periods, viz. those of the *Āraṇyaka*s, *Brāhmaṇa*s and *Veda*s and thus arrived at the date of 1200 BC for the last-named texts. However, when his own contemporaries, like Whitney, Goldstucker and Wilson, raised objections to this kind of ad-hocism, he threw his hands up, by saying (in his Preface to the *Ṛigveda*):

> I have repeatedly dwelt on the merely hypothetical character of the dates, which I have ventured to assign to the first periods of Vedic literature. All I have claimed for them has been that they are minimum dates, and that the literary productions of each period which either still exist or which formerly existed could hardly be accounted for within shorter limits of time than those suggested.

And then came his final surrender (Max Muller 1890, reprint 1979):

> If now we ask how we can fix the dates of these periods, it is quite clear that we cannot hope to fix a *terminum a qua* [sic]. **Whether the Vedic hymns were composed [in] 1000 or 1500 or 2000 or 3000 BC, no power on earth will ever determine.**

The great pity is that in spite of such a categorical declaration by Max Muller himself, his blind followers even today swear by 1200 BC as the date of the *Ṛigveda*. And this has led to immense confusion, as we shall presently see.

Thus, when in the 1920s the Harappan Civilization was discovered and dated to the third millennium BC (on the basis of the occurrence of some Harappan antiquities in already dated contexts in Mesopotamia), it was assumed that, since the Vedic civilization (as per the theory of Max Muller) was only as old as 1200 BC, the Harappan Civilization could not have been that of the Sanskrit-speaking Vedic people. Since the only other major linguistic group that existed in India was that of the Dravidian-speaking people, it was but natural for Marshall and his colleagues to hold that the Harappan Civilization belonged to these latter people.

Then came the climax. In 1946, Mortimer Wheeler carried out further excavations at Harappa and found a fortification-wall around one of the mounds at the site. Interpreting his discovery, he declared (Wheeler 1947: 82):

> The Āryan invasion of the Land of the Seven Rivers, the Punjab and its environs, constantly assumes the form of an onslaught upon the walled cities of the aborigines. For these cities the term used in the *Ṛigveda* is *pur*, meaning a 'rampart', 'fort' or 'stronghold' .... Indra, the Āryan War-god, is *puraṁdara*, 'fort-destroyer'. He shatters 'ninety forts' for his Āryan protege Divodāsa.
>
> Where are — or were — these citadels? It has in the past been supposed that they were mythical, or were 'merely places of refuge against attack, ramparts of hardened earth with palisades and a ditch'. The recent excavation of Harappa may be thought to have changed the picture. Here we have a highly evolved civilization of essentially non-Āryan type, now known to have employed massive fortifications, and known also to have dominated the river-system of north-western India at a time not distant from the likely period of the earlier Āryan invasions of that region. What destroyed this firmly-settled civilization? Climatic, economic, political deterioration may have weakened it, but its ultimate **extinction** is more likely to have been completed by deliberate and large-scale destruction. It may be no mere chance that at a late period of Mohenjo-daro men, women and children appear to have been massacred there. **On circumstantial evidence, Indra stands accused**. (Emphasis added.)

A close scrutiny of Wheeler's conclusions shows that these are ill-founded. For instance, take the massacre theory. During the nine years of excavation at Mohenjo-daro, altogether thirty-seven skeletons, some fragmentary and some complete, had been found. All these came from the Lower Town, where the commoners lived. None came from the Citadel, the seat of government. One really wonders why the 'invaders' spared the rulers. Anyway, the more important point is that **these skeletons came from different stratigraphic horizons**: some from Intermediate levels, some from late ones, while yet some others from deposits which accumulated after the abandonment of the site. If these people had died as a result of an invasion, one expects that the skeletons would all be there in one stratum and that would naturally be the uppermost since after that the site is said to have been abandoned. Added to the foregoing is the fact that a few of **the skeletons bore cut-marks that had healed**. Such a healing up is unlikely had the persons concerned died in a (supposed) warfare, for the death would have been almost immediate, without leaving a long interval for the wounds to heal. And finally, **no material remains whatsoever have been found at the site indicative of any warfare or even otherwise associable with any aliens**. Taking into account these and various other factors, one is inclined to agree with George F. Dales (1964) when he called this as a 'mythical massacre'. **Indeed, Indra stands exonerated!**

Here it may not be out of place to quote the comments of another eminent archaeologist, Colin Renfrew, on Wheeler's hypothesis of Aryan invasion. Says he (1988: 188 and 190):

> When Wheeler speaks of 'the Aryan invasion of the Land of the Seven Rivers, the Panjab', he has no warranty at all, so far as I can see. If one checks the dozen references in the *Ṛigveda* to the Seven Rivers, **there is nothing in any of them that to me implies invasion.**
>
> **...Despite Wheeler's comments, it is difficult to see what is particularly non-Aryan about the Indus Valley Civilization.** (Emphasis added.)

I do not propose discussing here whether the Harappans were a Dravidian-speaking or Sanskrit-speaking people. I have dealt with this question in great detail in a paper which forms part of a book being brought out by a Harvard University scholar. All that I would like to mention is that the various objections raised against an Harappan-Aryan equation are ill-founded. It is highly misleading to say that the Vedic Aryans were nomads. The *Ṛigveda* itself throws valuable light on the polity of the times, as indicated by the occurrence in it of such terms as ***sabhā, samiti, samrāṭ, rājan, rājaka***, etc. The first two terms clearly refer to assemblies that took vital decisions on matters of public interest, while the latter three terms point to a hierarchy of rulers. **In *RV* 6.27.8, Abhyāvartī Chāyamāna is referred to as a Samrāṭ, whereas in *RV* 8.21.18 Chitra is said to be a mere Rājan and the epithet of other still inferior rulers is Rājaka.** Does one expect such fine distinction of governance in a nomadic society? That these distinctions are not imaginary, as is likely to be argued by the 'nomad'-theory-protagonists, but real is borne out by the *Śatapatha Brāhmaṇa* (V.1.1.12-13) when it clearly states: ***avaram hi rājyam param Sāmrājyam***, which means that **the office of Rājan is lower and that of Samrāt, the higher.**

The mention of armours and forts clearly points to the high-level military strategy of the Aryans. Thus, for example, *RV* 10.101.8 mentions:

.... varma sīvyadhvam bahulā prithūni
puraḥ Kriṇudhvamāyasīradhṛiṣṭā

Stitch ye [oh gods] **the coats of armour, wide and many, make strong forts as of metal, safe from all assailants.**

In Verse *RV* 7.15.14, the devotee further prays that the **fort should have a hundred arms:** '*pūrbhavā śatabhujiḥ*'. Is this the prayer of a nomad?

The Vedic Aryans were well up on the economic front too. As indicated by *RV* 9.33.6, they were engaged in even sea-trade:

rāyaḥ Samudrāñschaturo asmabhyam soma viśvatah. Ā pavasva sahasriṇaḥ

O Soma, from every side pour forth four seas filled with a thousand-fold riches.

In order to carry out efficiently the sea-trade, the Vedic Aryans used sizeable boats which had as many as a hundred (i.e. a very large number of) oars. This is indicated by the following verse (*RV* 1.116.5):

anārambhaṇe tadvīrayethāmanāsthāne agrabhaṇe samudre
yadaśvinā ūhathurbhujyumastam ***śatāritrām nāvamātasthivānsam***

O Aśvins, you saved Bhujyu (from drowning) in a deep sea where there was nothing to hold on, by lifting him up in **a boat that had a hundred oars** and sending him to his place. This was indeed a brave act of yours.

The foregoing few examples should leave no doubt in the mind of anyone that, far from being nomads, the Vedic Aryans had reached a very advanced social, political and economic stage. Even the much-touted argument about the absence of the horse from the Harappan Civilization has no validity in the light of the new evidence that is turning up about its presence. The noted international authority on the palaeontology of the horse, Sandor Bokonyi of the Archaeological Institute, Budapest, had communicated to the Director General Archaeological Survey of India, through a letter in 1993, that **'the domestic nature of the Surkotada horse [a Harappan site in Kachchh] is undoubtful'** (Fig. 3.26). The terracotta model of the horse, found by Mackay in his excavations at Mohenjo-daro, is displayed in the National Museum, New Delhi. Lothal, the famous Harappan site in Gujarat, has also yielded a terracotta figure of the horse (Fig. 3.27). (For a fuller treatment of the subject, see Lal 1998: 109-12.)

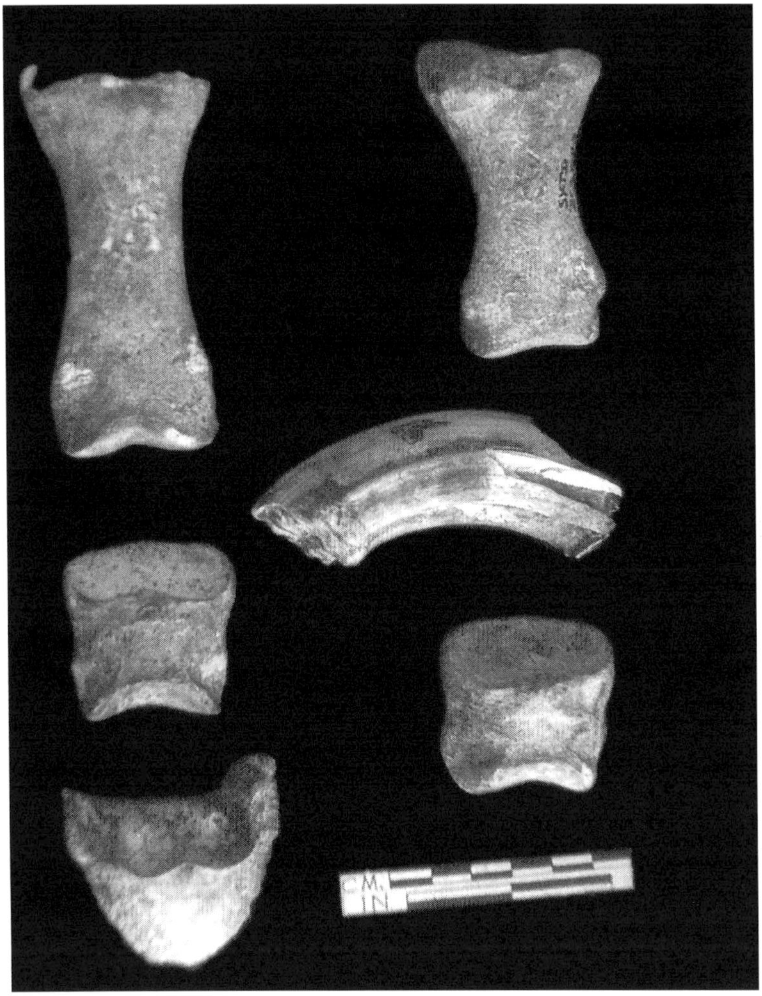

Fig. 3.26 Surkotada: Horse bones. Mature Harappan

There is yet another argument which is often advanced against an Aryan-Harappan equation. This relates to the spoked wheel which is referred to in the Vedic texts but is stated to be absent during the Harappan times. Echoing the views of a host of scholars of his ilk, both Western and Indian, says R. S. Sharma (1999: 18-19):

> There is no evidence for a spoked wheel at Harappa or Mohenjodaro where all the toy-carts found so far have solid wheels. Banawali in Hissar district in Haryana is associated with the use of the spoked wheels in the Harappan phase. According to its excavator, R.S. Bisht, a shard depicts a canopied cart with spoked wheels. But the painted shard produced by him shows seventeen parallel lines which appear to be decorative. These lines cannot be considered spokes, for neither they converge at a hub/central point nor do the distances between them tend to narrow down towards any end.

Well argued, Professor Sharma. But here is reproduced (Fig. 3.28) a

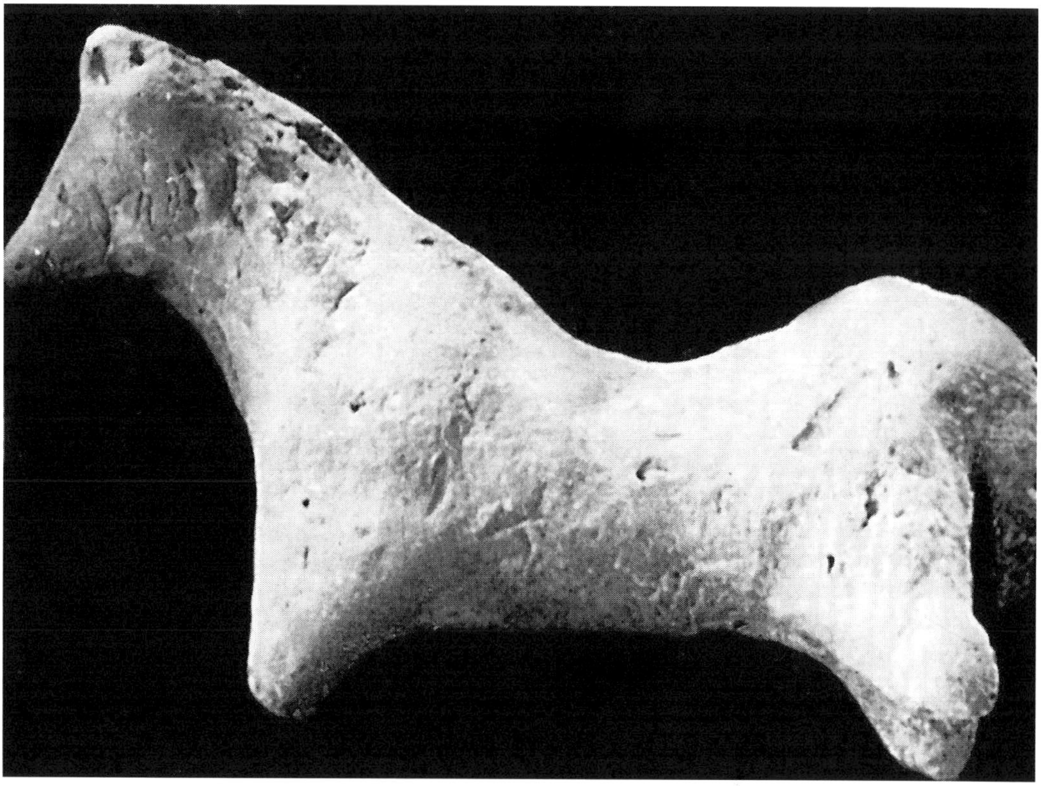

Fig. 3.27 Lothal: Terracotta horse. Mature Harappan

painted terracotta wheel from the Harappan levels of Rakhigarhi in Haryana, which clearly sets aside Sharma's above-mentioned objections. The painted **lines do converge at the central hub, and thus leave no doubt whatsoever about their representing the spokes of the wheel**. However, if the above example does not satisfy the learned professor, another example is reproduced from Kalibangan, a well-known Harappan site in Rajasthan (Fig. 3.29), in which too the painted lines converge at a central hub. And in case Professor Sharma shrugs his shoulders at these two examples, arguing, though quite unconvincingly, that the spokes are shown by merely painted lines, let me reproduce two examples from Banawali, in which the spokes are not painted but are shown in **low relief** (Fig. 3.30). Those who are conversant with the archaeology of the Early Historical period of India cannot fail to recall that

Fig. 3.28 Rakhigarhi: Terracotta wheel. The painted lines radiating from the central hub and reaching the circumference clearly represent the spokes of the wheel. Mature Harappan

Fig. 3.29 Kalibangan: Like the Rakhigarhi example, this terracotta wheel too is painted, depicting spokes. Mature Harappan

Fig. 3.30 Banawali: Terracotta wheels showing the spokes in low relief. The specimen on the left is worn out but the spokes may still be seen. The specimen on the right, though broken, shows the spokes very clearly. Mature Harappan

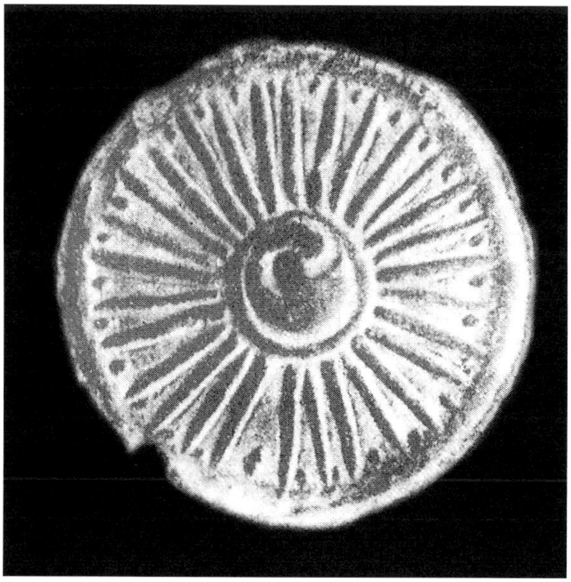

Fig. 3.31 Hastināpura: Terracotta wheel, showing spokes in low relief. Śuṅga-Kushan times

this very technique, viz. that of showing the spokes in low relief, was employed during the Śuṇga-Kushan times (see Lal 1954 & 1955: pl. XLVIII, no. 4; here Fig. 3.31).

At this point it may be well worth while to examine the relationship between the Harappan Civilizaiton and the *Ṛigveda* from an altogether different angle, viz. that of time-cum-space. Earlier (p.22) we had noted that the geomorphological, archaeological and radiocarbon dating evidences combine to show that the Sarasvatī dried up around 2000 BC. In Chapter I (p.2), we also noted that during the Ṛigvedic times the Sarasvatī was a highly active river, sometimes even breaking its banks. All this clearly shows that the *Ṛigveda* must antedate 2000 BC. By how many centuries, it is anyone's guess. Further, the geographical area covered by the Ṛivedic people, as given in *RV* 10.75, lay from the Gaṅgā-Yamunā on the east to the Indus on the west.

A simple question may now be posed: Which archaeolgical culture occupied the above-mentioned region during the period prior to 2000 BC? the **inescapable** answer is: it was the Harappan Civilization. Isn't it?

However, in spite of the fact that the various objections against a *Ṛigveda*-Harappan equation are petering out in thin air and that there is a very reasonable case for upholding that equation, I for one would like to plead for patiently awaiting the decipherment of the Harappan script. It is needless to add that, in spite of so many tall claims made by scholars from all over the world, no one has yet hit the mark (see Lal 1997: 203-14).

Anyway, leaving aside the Aryan-Harappan equation, the main point that had emerged from the still earlier paragraphs was, to repeat, that **there was**

no 'extinction' of the Harappan Civilization, as propagated by Wheeler (above, p.69) and orchestrated by others.

At Mohenjo-daro itself, which was claimed by Wheeler to have been the site of the 'massacre', there is a case for transition to what is known as the Jhukar complex. The same kind of devolution has been noted at Amri in Sindh. At Harappa there is yet another model of localized transformation: from the Harappan to the Cemetery H complex. This is also the case in Cholistan. In Gujarat there was yet another localized transformation — from the Harappan to what has been termed as the Rangpur complex. This is perfectly clear from the evidence of Rangpur. **Thus, in the entire area occupied by the Harappan Civilization we have a scenario of *continuity and not of any break*.** And an understanding of this important fact is necessary for appreciating the great truth that the Harappan Culture stands out as the prime source of the subsequent Indian culture.

In this context it may be well worth while quoting from a paper sent to this author in 1998 by Jim G. Shaffer and Diane Lichtenstein, both from USA (in press):

> A few scholars have proposed that there is nothing in the 'literature' firmly placing the Indo-Aryans ..... outside of South Asia, and now archaeological record is confirming this. ... As data accumulate to support cultural continuity in South Asian prehistoric and historic periods, a considerable restructuring of existing interpretive paradigms must take place. **We reject most strongly the simplistic historical interpretations, which date back to the eighteenth century, that continue to be imposed on South Asian culture history. These still prevailing interpretations are significantly diminished by European ethnocentrism, colonialism, racism and antisemitism.**

Here it may not be out of place to bring in also another kind of collateral evidence. It comes from archaeo-biology. After a detailed study of a large number of pre- and proto-historic skeletons, Hemphill and his colleagues came to the following conclusion (1991: 137):

> As for the question of biological continuity within the Indus Valley, two discontinuities appear to exist. The first occurs between 6000 and 4500 BC ... The second occurs at some point after 800 BC but before 200 BC.

It is thus abundantly clear that there was a ***biological continuity of the***

people themselves **even after the decline of the Mature Harappan cultural stage. And this explains the cultural continuity** which we shall deal with in detail in Chapter IV.

(V) THE LATE HARAPPAN SCENARIO IN THE SARASVATĪ VALLEY AND BEYOND

The reader may have noticed that while dealing with the occupational strata at Kalibangan, Banawali and Rakhigarhi, no reference was made to a Late Harappan stage. All these sites were abandoned when the Mature Harappan was still ongoing. Neither Kalibangan nor Rakhigarhi was occupied once it was deserted, while the subsequent occupation at Banawali came up at a much later stage.

When did this desertion take place? The radiocarbon dates for Kalibangan indicate that the site may have been abandoned around 1900 BC. The evidence from Banawali suggests that the desertion of the site may have been somewhat later. There are no radiocarbon dates yet for Rakhigarhi. All told, it appears that these sites, located in the Sarasvatī–Dṛiṣadvatī basin, were given up some time in the first quarter of the second millennium BC.

But why? While there is yet no scientifically established reason in the cases of Banawali and Rakhigarhi, there is enough to go by in the case of Kalibangan. The bores made by Raikes, a hydrologist, in the bed of the Ghaggar adjacent to the site of Kalibangan have shown that it was the drying up of the river that resulted in the abandonment of the site. In fact, the very title of his paper is telling: 'Kalibangan: Death from Natural Causes' (Raikes 1968). Earlier, while discussing the fate of the glacial-fed Sarasvatī, we referred to the findings of two renowned geologists, Puri and Verma (1998), who have shown that a major tectonic upheaval in the Himalayan region resulted in the diversion of the waters of the Sarasvatī into the Yamunā system (above, p.24). This considerably reduced the water-supply in the Sarasvatī basin, the inhabitants having been left to subsist on local rains and limited water-supply that the greatly attenuated river brought from the Siwalik foothills. The obvious result was the migration of the people towards the north-east where some water was still available in the uppermost reaches of the Sarasvatī and Ghaggar and further east in the upper plains of the Gaṅgā–Yamunā *Doāb*. In these areas there are many sites representing this migration of the Harappans, but we shall take up here only two, namely Hulas and Alamgirpur.

Located close to the Katha Nala, which joins the Yamunā, Hulas lies in Saharanpur District of Uttar Pradesh. While it covers an area of 330 x 170 metres, the excavation revealed that the Late Harappan occupation was very limited in extent (Dikshit 1982). Likewise, of the 5-m thick vertical deposit, only the lowermost 1.5 m is ascribable to the Late Harappan times. (The rest belonged successively to the Painted Grey Ware, Northern Black Polished Ware periods, and so on, with which we are not concerned here.) That the lowermost occupation is genetically connected with the Mature Harappan is clearly established by the discovery in it of a terracotta sealing bearing a typical Harappan inscription. But the glorious Mature Harappan scenario was no more there: no cardinally oriented houses, no public drains, no monumental buildings, and so on. Only some mud-brick platforms are reminiscent of their Harappan counterparts. This transition from the Mature to Late stage is best reflected in the pottery at Hulas. While one does meet with the familiar dishes-on-stand and vases, there are clearly perceivable changes in their features. Thus, for example, the dish component of the former begins to have a pronounced drooping rim or the vases an elongated neck (Fig. 3.32). There is also a proliferation of miniature pots. Amongst the painted designs, while the Mature Harappan diagnostic ones like the peacock and banana leaf are still there, some new ones also make their appearance.

The other site, Alamgirpur, is located on the bank of the Hindon, a tributary of the Yamunā, in Meerut District of Uttar Pradesh. Though it has not yielded any seal or sealing (the excavation was doubtless limited, Y.D. Sharma in *Indian Archaeology 1958-59 — A Review*, pp. 50-55), there is an inscription in the Harappan script on the base of a three-legged terracotta *chakalā* (also called *pāṭā*), used for rolling bread (Fig. 3.33). There were also the familiar cubical dice marked with 1 to 6 circlets on their respective faces, and the terracotta 'cakes'. But the changes noticed in the pottery at Hulas are reflected in the pottery at Alamgirpur as well. So the transition is more than apparent. There are other sites in the north-east region which show further dilution of the Mature Harappan features, for example Bhagwanpura (Joshi 1993). In any case, urbanism was a bygone story, and villages dominated the scene. As I have stated elsewhere also, these post-Urban Harappan villages must have proudly conveyed to one another their great sense of survival by

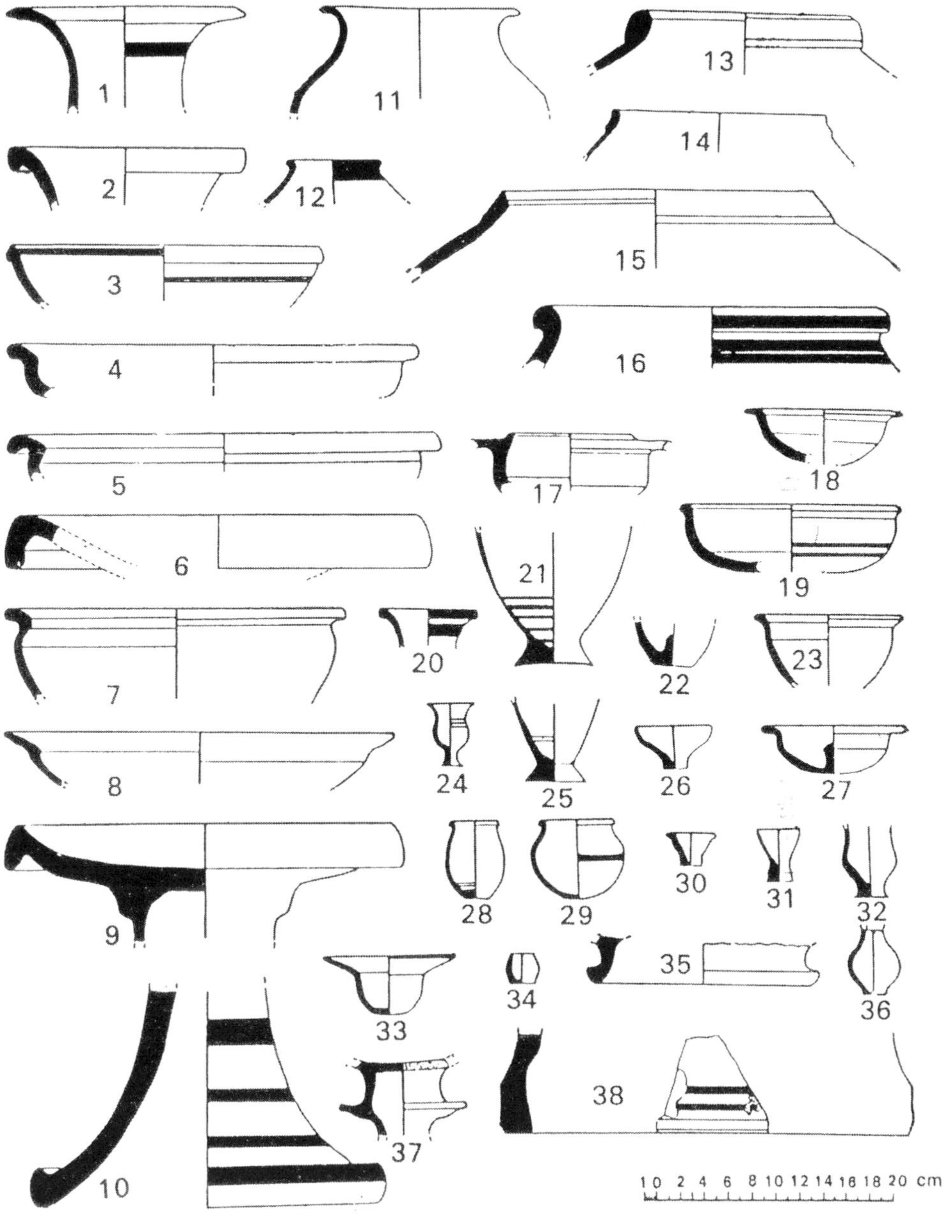

Fig. 3.32 Hulas: Pottery types. Late Harappan

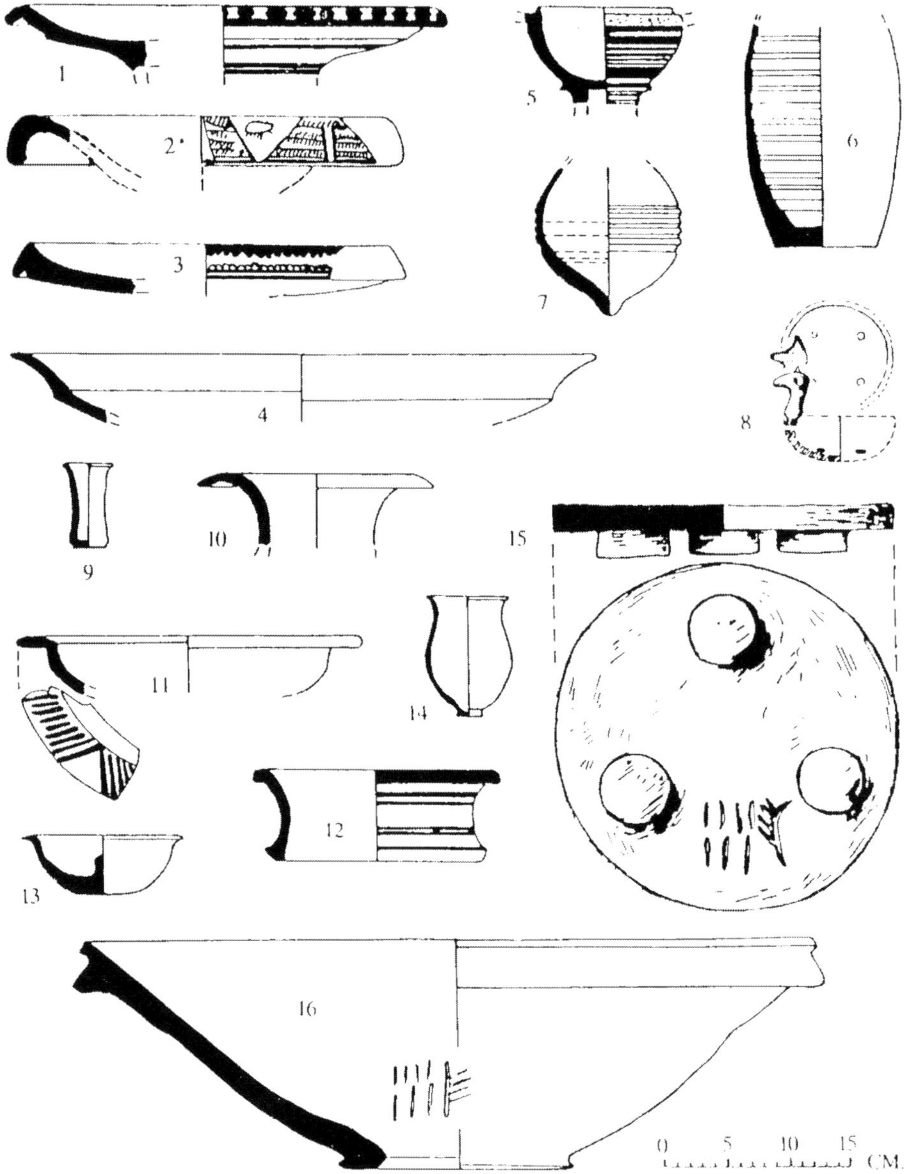

Fig. 3.33 Alamgirpur: Late Harappan pottery including a three-legged *chakalā* bearing an inscription on the underside

whispering: "C'ties may come c'ties may go, but we go on for ever" (after Tennyson's *The Brook*).

As times passed, there was more and more dilution but many of the non-urban features of the Harappan Civilization which were deep-rooted in the masses continued through the subsequent millennia and are easily observable even today in the country. This aspect of the continuity of Indian culture will be dealt with in some detail in the chapter that follows.

CHAPTER IV

THE CULTURAL STREAM FLOWS ON

While assessing cultural continuity down the ages in India, it has to be remembered that the face of the country has been changing fast, particularly since the middle of the twentieth century. With growing industrialization, people are moving in large numbers from rural areas to urban centres. Further, because of differences in the earning levels of the various members of any given family, familial bonds are breaking up. This has affected the house-plans even in villages where once there used to be large, usually single-storeyed family houses of a particular pattern to which we shall refer in detail a little later. Because of limited space, cities are growing more vertically than horizontally, presenting a jungle of concrete. To cap it all, with exposure through electronic media to the Western way of living, the old ways and consequently the articles involved therein are all gradually disappearing. (This is not an expression of any kind of lamentation, but merely a statement of facts. Doubtless, change is the very essence of life; non-change is stagnation and death.) Anyway, for a study of cultural continuity in India the rural-scape presents a better ground, even though there too the scenario is changing and is not the same as it used to be say fifty years ago: for example, the ploughshare is giving way to tractors, or the drawing up of water from the wells by means of large animal-skin bags, pulled up by a pair of bullocks, to electrically operated water-pumps. Nevertheless, there is quite a lot which can be easily identified and in the following pages we shall deal with it.

(I) ORNAMENTS, MAKE-UP AND TOILETRY

In the concluding part of the Preface I had stated that the reader should not be taken aback if he discovers that the practice of applying *sindūra* (vermilion) to the *māṅga* (line of partition of the hair on the head) by married Hindu women goes back to the Early Harappan times. This startling evidence comes from some terracotta female figurines, found in levels dating back to 2800-2600 BC

Fig. 4.1a

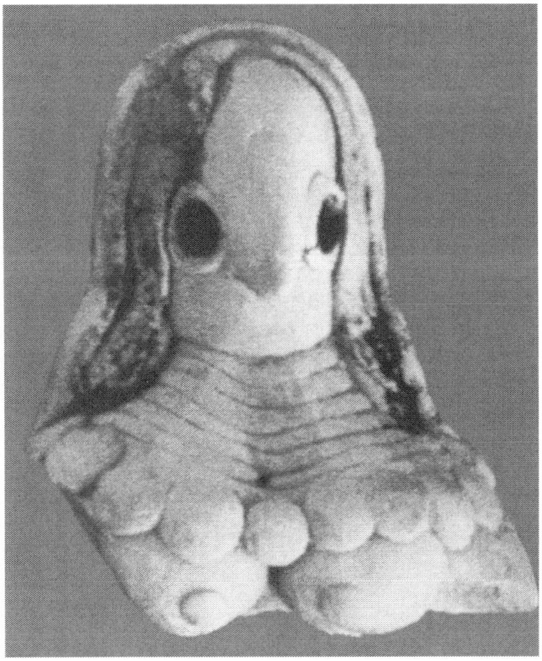

Fig. 4.1b

Fig. 4.1a & b Nausharo: Terracotta female figures, painted. The yellow colour on ornaments suggests that these were made of gold; the hair is black, while the red on the line of partition of the hair indicates the use of vermilion. Period IB, 2800-2600 BC

at Nausharo and at Mehrgarh, both in Pakistan, by J.-F. Jarrige and his colleagues (Jarrige *et al.* 1979 and in press). The figures are painted with three colours (Figs. 4.1a & b). While the body has the usual terracotta colour, the ornaments are painted in yellow so as to indicate that these were made of gold. The hair is painted black which is its usual colour. But what is most exciting is the application of red colour to the medial parting line of the hair. This clearly represents vermilion (*sindūra*) which is even today applied by married Hindu women at the same location (the *māṅga*; see Fig. 4.2). Although it is unbelievable that this practice had its roots in a cultural milieu nearly 5000 years ago, yet it is true. It has been well said that **tradition dies hard**, and specially so when it relates to the womenfolk who have always been the bulwark of cultural continuity.

Fig. 4.2 Bihar Chief Minister Shrimati Rabri Devi and her husband Shri Laloo Prasad Yadava, in the State capital, Patna. Mark the vermilion in the *māṅga* of the lady, which is an indicator of her marital status

Since we have started with the womenfolk, let us continue to deal with the various items relating to them. Like me, the reader too will feel surprised that almost every kind of Harappan jewellery has come down to us, evidently on account of the charm it wielded and the fondness of our womenfolk for the same.

Fig. 4.3 shows a hollow cone of gold, discovered at Mohenjo-daro. This ornament is used even now on the head by women in Rajasthan and Haryana (Fig. 4.4) and is called *chauk* in Hindi. Referring to it Vats (1940: 442) states: 'By Hindus in northern India *chauk*s are regarded among the essential ornaments which every man, rich or poor, has to give at the wedding of his daughter-

Fig. 4.3 Mohenjo-daro: Gold cone. Mature Harappan

Fig. 4.4 A newly married lady, on the right, wearing a conical ornament on the head (covered by the *dupattā*). She also wears bangles all over her right arm

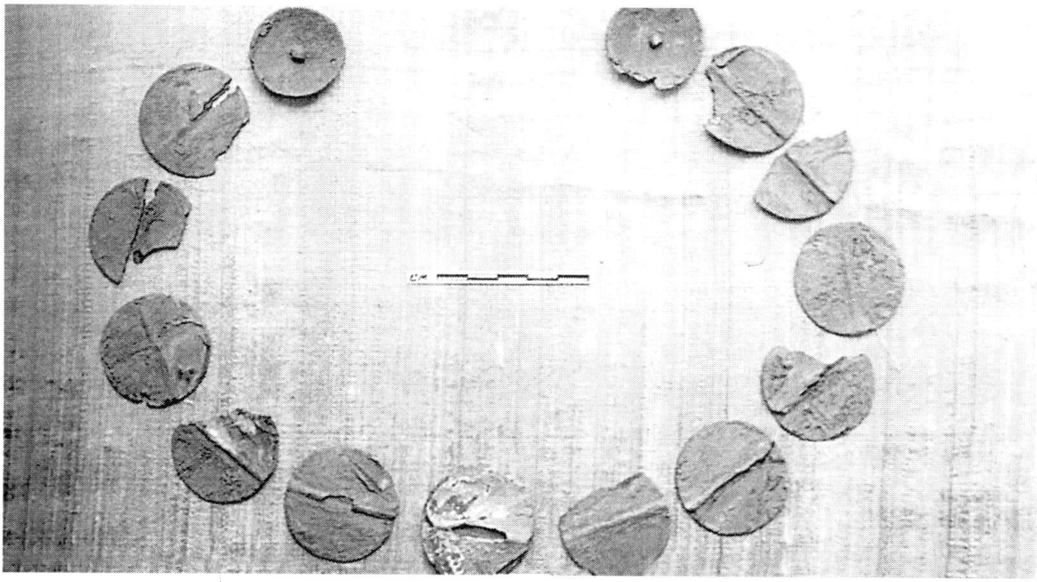

Top : Fig. 4.5 Kunal: Discular beads of silver, having perforation along the diameter. Early Harappan

Bottom right : Fig. 4.6 Lothal: Discular beads of gold, having perforation along the diameter. Mature Harappan

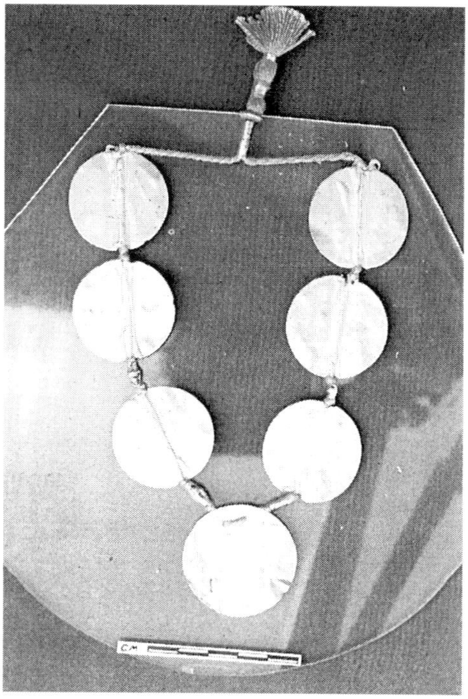

in-law. This ornament is now worn chiefly on religious and important domestic ceremonies only.'

Since necklaces have been worn by women the world over, one may not find them of any special significance. But necklaces consisting of beads of a particular shape and perforation do call for special attention. In this case the beads are discular in shape and perforated along the diameter. Fig. 4.5 shows such beads in silver, from the Early Harappan levels (ca. 3000-2800 BC) of Kunal in Haryana,

Top left : Fig. 4.7 Mohenjo-daro: The famous bronze figure of a 'dancing girl', wearing spiralled bangles on the upper left arm. Mature Harappan

Bottom left : Fig. 4.8 Kunal: Spiralled bangles, silver. Early Harappan

Top right : Fig. 4.9 A woman wearing spiralled bangles

while Fig. 4.6 depicts the same type in gold from a Mature Harappan stratum at Lothal. Necklaces comprising discular beads are worn even now in certain parts of northern India. While one cannot but be attracted by the necklace dangling between the breasts of the 'dancing girl' from Mohenjo-daro, what is significant in terms of continuity is the set of spiralled bangles worn by her on the upper left arm (Fig. 4.7). This kind of bangles, on the one hand, goes back even to the Early Harappan times (at Kunal, in silver, Fig. 4.8), and, on the other, comes down to the present (Fig. 4.9). Another arm-ornament which needs to be noted in this context is the wristlet with hour-glass (*ḍamaru*-like) shape. This is engraved on a stone stele from Banawali in Haryana, found in the Harappan levels. This kind of wrist-ornament continues to be worn by the womenfolk in Rajasthan and Gujarat. The wearing of a girdle (called *karadhanī* or *petī* in Hindi) around the waist, observed in the case of so many Harappan terracotta female figurines, may be seen even today amongst the womenfolk in rural areas. In cities, the Hindu women in northern India wear this ornament when they bedeck themselves on the occasion of *Karawā chauth*, a fast-cum-festival observed by the ladies praying for long life of their husband. Worn around the ankle by the Harappan women was the *pāyala* which too may be seen in the villages. Out of sheer fancy, some girls in cities may also be seen now and then wearing a somewhat sophisticated version of this ornament.

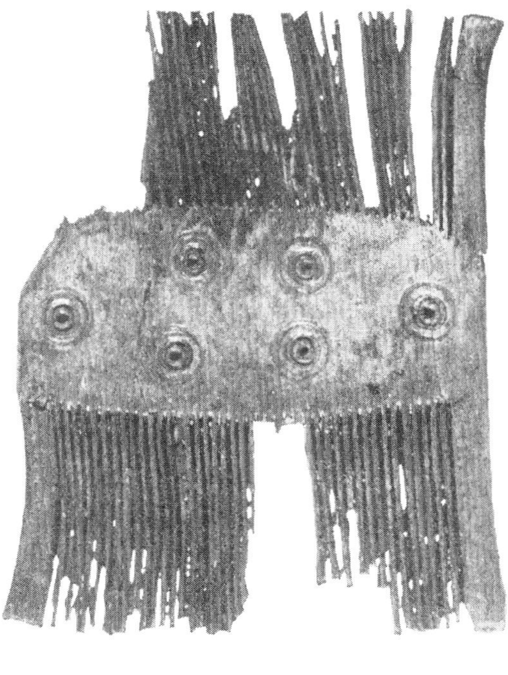

Fig. 4.10 Mohenjo-daro: Ivory comb with teeth on two opposite sides. Mature Harappan

In the context of gold ornaments, it needs to be specially mentioned that at Banawali was found a 'touchstone bearing gold streaks of different hues' (Bisht

1987: 150). This was evidently used to test the purity of gold. Is it not exciting that the same method is applied by the goldsmiths even to this day?

We may now pass on from ornaments to objects of toiletry. Combs have been used all over the world for doing the hair. But the Harappans used a special kind of comb which was squarish in shape and had 'teeth' on two opposite sides (Fig. 4.10). The teeth are somewhat thick on one side but finer on the other. Exactly the same kind of comb has been in use in rural India until recently and may be seen even now in some wayside markets. It is called *kakai* in the Bundelkhand region and is different from the *kanghā* (comb) which is elongated and has the teeth only on one side. Collyrium was applied to the eyes even during the Early Harappan times (2800-2500 BC), as revealed by a terracotta figurine from Nausharo. While this figure is male, there is no

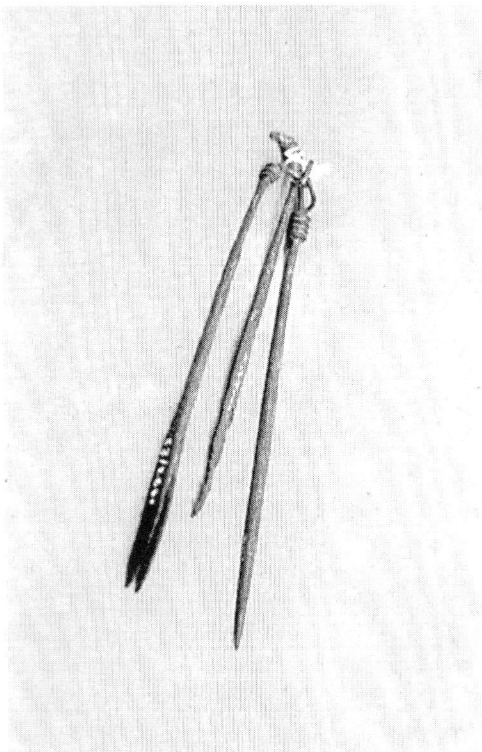

Fig. 4.11 Harappa: A three-in-one toiletry gadget, copper. Mature Harappan

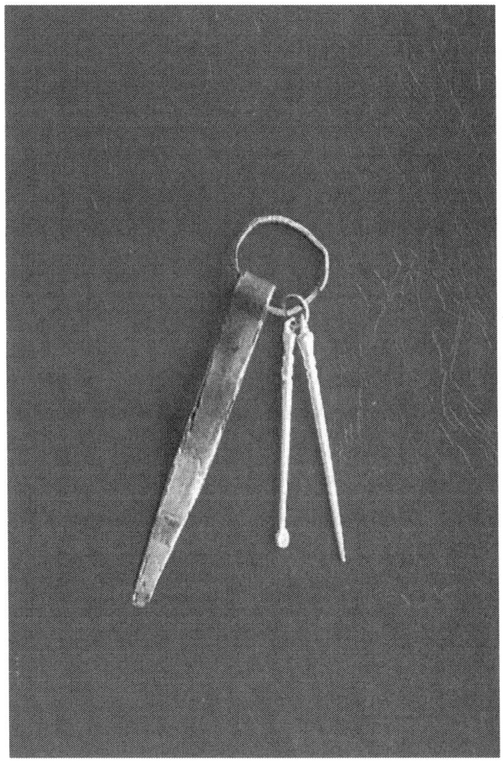

Fig. 4.12 A modern three-in-one toiletry gadget, copper

reason to think that the womenfolk did not use collyrium. The use of collyrium is in vogue even today and more interestingly the modern collyrium stick is also similar to that used by the Harappans. In both cases, these are made of metal. The Harappan nail-parer, with a flat and sharp cutting end, has also been continuing, though, of late, it is being replaced by a new kind of gadget. Prior to the coming into being of glass mirrors, metallic mirrors were in use in our country. These were circular in shape and were provided with a handle. This type may be seen in medieval sculptures and paintings. The circular surface was highly polished so that one could easily see one's face in it. This type of metallic mirror is as old as the Harappan times. But all these similarities pale into insignificance when we have a look at a three-in-one toiletry gadget. At Harappa was found a trio made of copper. It consists of a tweezer, a small pointed rod and a somewhat flattish object Fig. (4.11). A similar three-in-one piece in metal is available even today in the market (Fig. 4.12). Enquiry reveals that the tweezer is used for plucking small-sized hair that sometimes grows on the inner side of the eyelids and is thus a source of irritation. The small pointed rod is meant for cleaning spaces between the teeth. The third object in the modern set has sometimes a small cup at its end which is used for removing wax from inside the ears. All told, the concept of three-in-one is indeed striking.

(II) GAMES AND RECREATION

We may now pass on to objects relating to games and recreation. The Harappan children played with rattles, whistles, tops (*phirkinīs*), hop-scotch discs, all of terracotta, but must have specially enjoyed wearing masks. Similar terracotta objects are used by children today, specially in the villages. Kenoyer has published a photograph of children at Harappa playing the game called *piṭṭu*, with discs made from broken pottery, alongside similar specimens found in the excavations at the ancient site (Kenoyer 1998: Figs. 7.16 and 7.17; here Figs. 4.13 and 4.14 respectively). In the Rakhigarhi excavations, such discs have been found in a stack (Fig. 4.15). Like the present children in the countryside, the Harappan children also enjoyed playing with such toys as bulls with mobile heads and monkeys that could be moved up and down along a rope. The Harappan adults seem to have taken to some brain-storming games like the chess, as suggested by Rao (1985: 503) on the basis of the occurrence of gamesmen (Figs. 4.16 and 4.17). However, because of the perishable nature

Fig. 4.13 Children at Harappa, playing with pottery discs the game called *piṭṭu*

Fig. 4.14 Harappa: Pottery discs from Mature Harappan levels

Fig. 4.15 Rakhigarhi: A stack of pottery discs, *in situ* in a Mature Harappan stratum

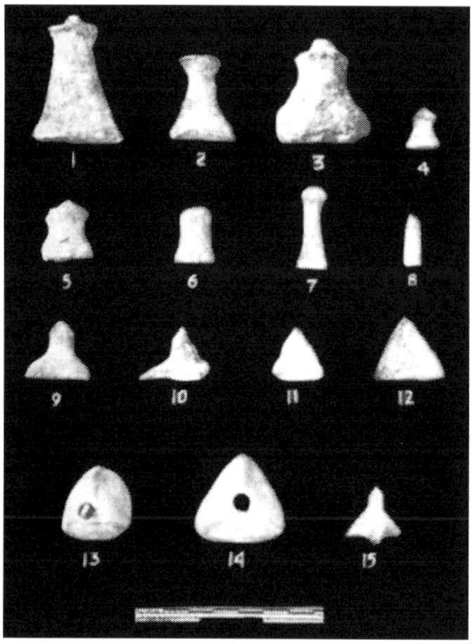

Fig. 4.16 Lothal: Terracotta gamesmen. Mature Harappan

Fig. 4.17 Use of gamesmen in chess; reconstruction by S.R. Rao. The Lothal gamesmen are on the left and the modern ones on the right

Fig. 4.18 Mohenjo-daro: Cubical dice in terracotta, with 1-6 blind holes on respective faces. Mature Harappan

Fig. 4.19 Modern examples of cubical dice, with 1-6 blind holes on respective faces

of its material, the board has not survived. No less interesting are cubical dice having 1, 2, 3, 4, 5 and 6 blind holes on the respective faces (Fig. 4.18). Similar gaming cubes are in use even today (Fig. 4.19).

Before we take up topics like house- and town-planning, agriculture, transport, religion, etc. we may refer to some less serious, yet interesting, items of pet animals and birds. Thus, would you believe that the Harappans too put a collar around the neck of their dogs (Fig. 4.20) or kept their birds in a cage (Fig. 4.21), just as we do now (Fig. 4.22).

Top left : Fig. 4.20 Mohenjo-daro: Terracotta dog, wearing a collar. Mature Harappan

Bottom left : Fig. 4.21 Harappa: Terracotta cage, with birds. Mature Harappan

Bottom right : Fig. 4.22 Modern example of keeping birds in a cage

(III) HOUSE- AND TOWN-PLANNING

In any part of the world and at any given time there has always been an economically differentiated society, and the Harappan times were no exception to this. Thus, while on the one hand there were very big houses of the elites, on the other there were hutments of the labour class consisting of a small room and a verandah in front. However, the middle class, comprising essentially agriculturists, had what may be called medium-sized houses, but with a characteristic layout. These consisted of a courtyard, on three sides of which there were rooms and the wall on the fourth side had a gate, opening on the street. This gate was pretty wide so as to allow easy entry of bullock-carts and cattle. In the courtyard there was sufficient space for parking the carts as well as for a cattle-shed. Further, for providing fodder and water to the cattle there were mud-brick troughs, usually 50-60 cm high, in which lower parts of large jars were affixed to hold water. A part of the courtyard was also kept reserved for cooking (to which we shall refer later). Sometimes there was a well also

Fig. 4.23 Kalibangan: Part of the fortification-wall around the citadel, showing alternate courses of headers and stretchers (now called the English bond). Mature Harappan

Fig. 4.24 Kalibangan: Successive floors of clay with soling of terracotta nodules and charcoal, in a house in Lower Town. Mature Harappan

in the courtyard. On either side of the entrance, on the exterior, there was a small platform on which the house-members and neighbours could just sit and chat or even discuss serious matters concerning the community. It is interesting to note that an identical planning of the house is still prevalent in the villages, even though concrete-made, courtyard-less, double storeyed houses, simulating the urban pattern, are also coming up. In any case, we noticed that in the 1960s when we were excavating at Kalibangan almost every house in the neighbouring village followed the aforementioned courtyard-pattern inclusive of the wide entrance, outside platforms (called *chabūtarā*s) and cattle-troughs. The only difference we noticed was that the occupants of these *chabūtarā*s smoked hookah (an Indian version of the tobacco-pipe) and discussed whom to vote and whom not to — things which evidently were not there during the Harappan times.

There are certain similarities between the Harappan times and now, even in the methods of construction and use of materials (forgetting, of course, the urban scenario). It looks strange, yet it is a fact that what is called the 'English bond' was in use during the Harappan times (Fig. 4.23). In this method, while constructing a wall, alternate courses consist of headers and stretchers. The roofs of the Harappan houses were flat and made by laying, at the top of the walls, horizontal beams and thatching material like canes, consolidated with mud. We noticed this composition in a fallen roof in a room in the southern part of the Lower Town at Kalibangan. This is precisely the manner in which the roofs were laid out in the neighbouring village when we were there. However, most remarkable was the method of laying out the floor during the

Harappan times at Kalibangan. Broken but hard-baked terracotta nodules, interspersed with charcoal, were first placed as the soling material. Over it was laid out a layer of clay. The floor was, of course, renovated as and when necessary (Fig. 4.24). When we encountered this kind of flooring in the excavation we just could not understand the reason behind such a composition. However, luckily for us some Public Works Department engineers once came to see the excavations. While showing them round the site we asked them about the reason for such a flooring. To our surprise, they shot back: 'There is nothing unusual about it. Even now we use this technique of providing a hard soling with intermixture of charcoal pieces in laying out the floors in areas where the soil is salty and the subsoil water-table is relatively high'. 'The presence of charcoal serves two purposes', they added. 'In the first place, it prevents the moisture from travelling up and thus saves the walls from the saline effects; otherwise they begin to crumble on account of saltpetre. Secondly, it acts against termites and this gives relief to the occupants from them'. Should we not salute the Kalibanganites for this 'indigenous' technology?

Harappan urban settlements were characterized by the orientation of streets along the cardinal directions, i. e. north-south and east-west (cf. Figs. 3.10, 12 and 13). Whether the same was true of Harappan rural sites is not known, since not much work has been done on them. Anyway, what is of interest is that not only even now some of the Indian settlements follow this pattern but during the Early Historical times, i.e. in the fourth-third century BC too, many settlements were laid out on this criss-cross pattern, for example Śiśupālgarh in Orissa (Lal 1949 and 1991). Square on plan and enclosed by a fortification-wall, Śiśupālgarh had eight gates, two on each side, which were connected with streets running north-south and east-west. And no less interesting is the fact that this kind of layout of the settlement finds mention in contemporary literature. However, it needs to be added that we do not yet have any examples of the period between the end of the Harappan times and the Early Historical.

(IV) COOKING AND ASSOCIATED ITEMS

It is most unbelievable that the *tandūr*, a typical cooking oven used in the north-western part of the Indian subcontinent, should date back to ca. 2800 BC. Examples have been met with in the Early Harappan levels of Kalibangan (Fig. 4.25). These were cylindrical in shape and plastered on the interior like

Fig. 4.25 Kalibangan: Clay *tandūrs* (cooking ovens). Early Harappan

their modern counterparts. In the somewhat late Harappan levels at Alamgirpur in Uttar Pradesh has been found a three-legged, circular *pāṭā* (also called *chakalā*) in terracotta (see Fig. 3.33, no. 15). Incidentally, it also bears an inscription in the Harappan script on the underside. Similar *pātās*, made of either wood or stone, are in use today for preparing bread (Fig. 4.26). For cutting firewood metal axes similar to the present ones were used. In fact, a model in terracotta also shows the manner in which the handle was inserted. The Harappan adze-axe, used for digging, is again similar to the present ones.

Fig. 4.26 A modern three-legged *pātā*, used for rolling bread

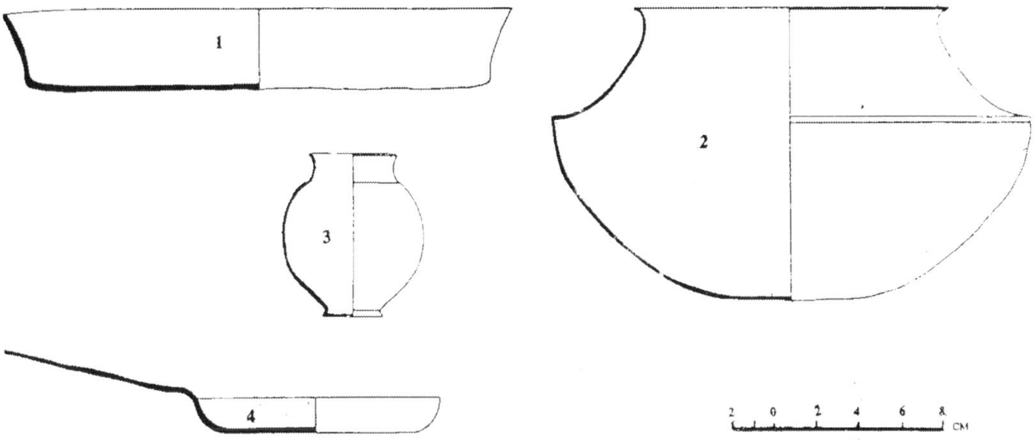

Fig. 4.27 Some Mature Harappan metal utensils

Many of the utensils used by the Harappans remind us of their modern counterparts in northern India, for example the handled frying pan, carinated *hāṇḍī*, high-edged *thālī* and *loṭā*, all made of copper (Fig. 4.27). Nowadays these are used respectively for frying something, cooking curries, eating food and drinking water. The *thālī* with raised edge is very popular with the labour class in eastern India where they quickly prepare *sattu* (Skt. *Saktu*) in it, eat it and rush on to their work. The Harappans used an oval cup with elongated nozzle for feeding babies with milk. Interestingly, the terracotta example from Kalibangan (Fig. 4.28) also bears the head of a cow. Similar cups, of metal, were used in rural areas for baby-feeding before the introduction of plastic

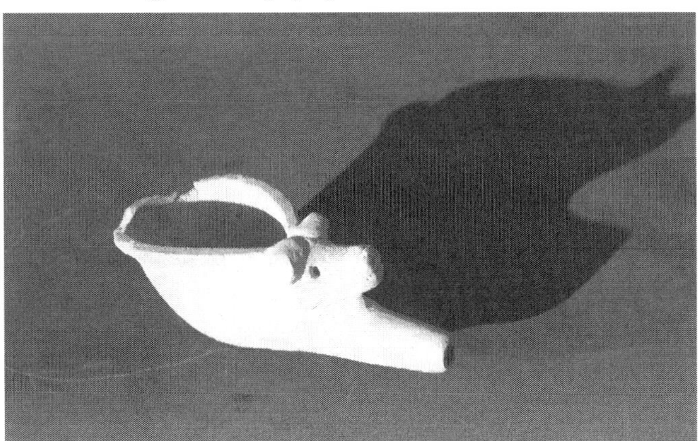

Fig. 4.28 Kalibangan: Terracotta feeding cup. Mature Harappan

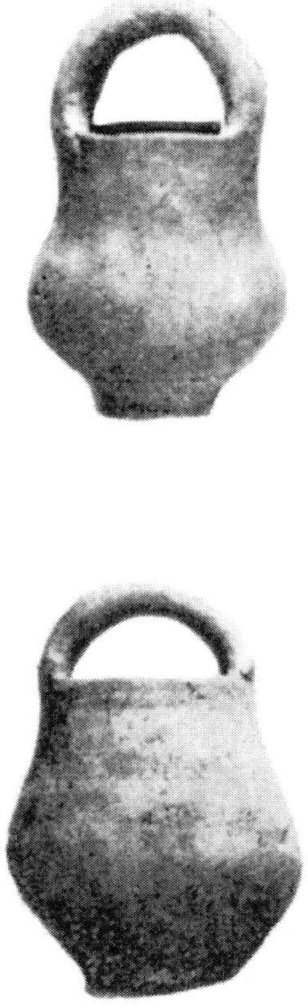

Fig. 4.29 Mohenjo-daro: Pottery *kamaṇḍalus*. Mature Harappan

Fig. 4.30 A Sādhū with a *kamaṇḍalu* by his side

bottles with rubber nipples. Last but not least, is it not surprising to find a *kamaṇḍalu*-shaped vessel in the Harappan repertoire (Fig. 4.29)? Do we then have to envisage some sādhūs (Fig. 4.30) as well in the Harappan population?

(V) AGRICULTURE AND WATER-MANAGEMENT

The excavations at Kalibangan, Banawali and Dholavira have brought to light some very noteworthy evidence regarding agriculture and water-supply. At Kalibangan were found the remains of a ploughed field, ascribable to the Early

Fig. 4.31 Kalibangan: An agricultural field, showing criss-cross pattern of the furrows. Early Harappan

Harappan times and datable to ca. 2800 BC. This field had two sets of furrows, one running north-south and the other east-west. The distance between the individual furrows in the former set was 1.9 m, whereas in the latter it was only 30 cm (Figs. 4.31 and 32). It is most interesting to note that this very pattern of ploughing the fields is still prevalent not only in northern Rajasthan, where Kalibangan is located (Fig. 4.33), but also in Haryana, Panjab and western Uttar Pradesh. At present, mustard is grown in the widely distanced (north-south) furrows and horse gram in the other (Fig. 4.34). It is most likely that the same crops were raised during the Early Harappan and Harappan times, since physical evidence for these items is available from the excavations. Prima facie, the whole thing looks like a simple case of continuity of a tradition. While that is no doubt so, there is something more in this kind of patterning of the furrows than meets the eye. Kalibangan, like most of the Harappan sites, is located in the northern hemisphere, well north of

Fig. 4.32 Kalibangan: Another view of the same field

Fig. 4.33 Around present Kalibangan village: The system of ploughing the field, which also has the criss-cross pattern of the furrows

the Tropic of Cancer. Hence in these areas the shadows fall to the north and during winters, the season in which the mustard and horse gram crops are raised, these shadows are still longer since the sun goes down to the southern hemisphere. And in here lies the point to be appreciated. The mustard plants are pretty tall and thus cast long shadows, whereas the horse gram plants are relatively much smaller and so are their shadows. Thus, by sowing the mustard plants in the north-south rows care is taken that their shadows fall more on one another rather than on the horse gram plants. **Had the mustard plants been sown in the east-west rows, their shadows would have completely covered the horse gram plants, depriving the latter of the sun's rays and consequently hampering their growth. Should not we take our hats off to our ancestors**

Fig. 4.34 Around present Kalibangan village: A field with mustard plants in the widely distanced furrows and those of horse gram in the others

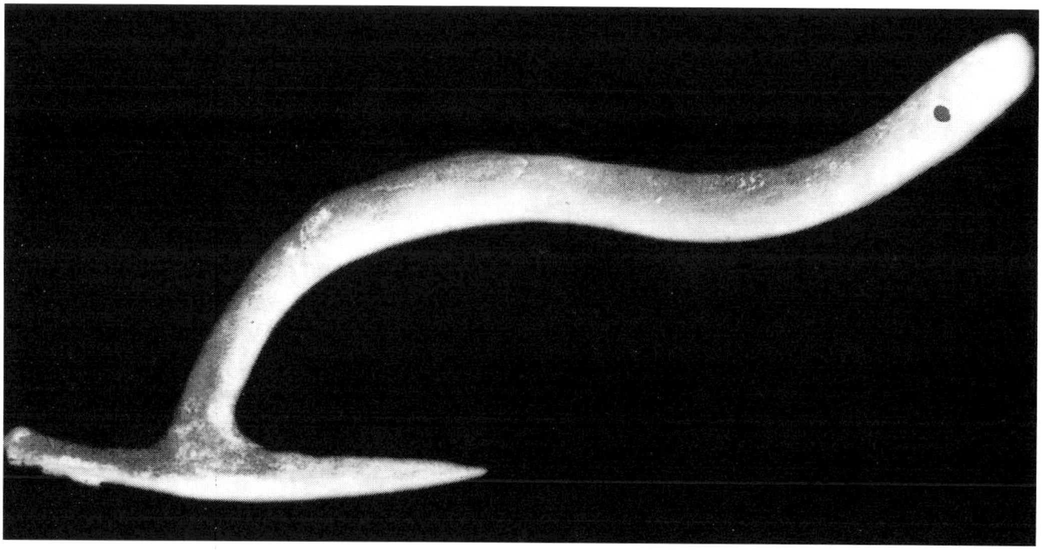

Fig. 4.35 Banawali: Terracotta model of a plough. Mature Harappan

five thousand years ago for having evolved this kind of crop-patterning?

Although terracotta models of ploughshares had been recovered from the excavations at Mohenjo-daro and Harappa, these were mostly broken and thus did not give a clear picture of what their complete shape was like. Banawali has now yielded a full specimen, in terracotta of course (Fig. 4.35). It consists of a curved beam and a sharpened 'shoe'. More or less similar ploughshares are still in use not only in Haryana, where Banawali is situated, but also in neighbouring Panjab and Rajasthan.

Interesting evidence has been obtained from Harappa in respect of the thrashing of grains. To the north of the Citadel, between the workmen's quarters and the granaries, have been discovered a series of circular pavements formed by four to five rings of kiln-fired bricks, set on edge. The central part, however, was found to be without any bricks, with the added evidence of a pit about 70 cm in depth (Fig. 4.36). This 'hollow' was continued upwards for about 40 cm. Around the central part were also found fragments of straw and husk. The location of these pavements not far from the granaries as well as their own features, coupled with the recovery of straw and husk therefrom, tend to suggest that the pavements were used for thrashing grains. It is a

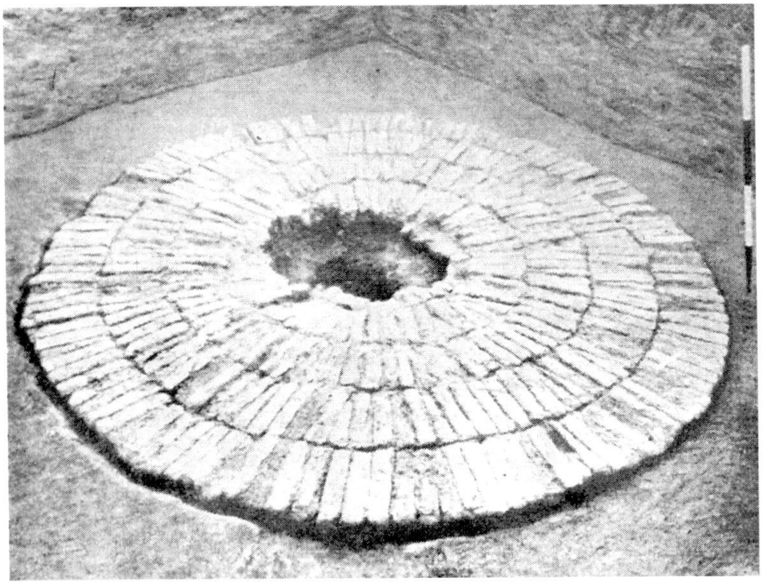

reasonable surmise that in the central hollow was inserted a wooden mortar which has since disappeared. Perhaps two workmen handled a pestle, also of wood, and alternately thrashed the grain inside the mortar. While Fig. 4.37 shows a modern example from Kashmir, similar pounding system prevails in many other regions of northern India.

For the supply of water there were wells within the courtyard of the house. These had a lining of wedge-shaped bricks (Fig. 4.38). Most probably the womenfolk used to draw the water out, as is the practice even today in the villages. But Dholavira has yielded evidence which suggests that where the water-table was very low, the water was drawn up through leather bags with the help of

Top left: Fig. 4.36 Harappa: Platform of kiln-fired bricks. In the central hollow was fixed a wooden mortar for pounding grains. Mature Harappan

Bottom left: Fig. 4.37 Near Srinagar (Kashmir): Pounding rice with pestles in a wooden mortar

Fig. 4.38 Kalibangan: A well, lined with wedge-shaped bricks, in the courtyard of a house. Mature Harappan

bullocks. Fig. 4.39 shows a stone-lined well with a stone trough on one side. The basal slab of the trough bears abrasion marks left by the rope that constantly rubbed against it, which is what is observed also in the modern examples too. Fig. 4.40 shows an artist's reconstruction of the process.

The wide flood-plains of the Sarasvati, Indus, Ravi, etc. on which the Harappan sites were located provided enough silt for agricultural purposes. However, some scholars are of the view that there were irrigation canals as well. While much more evidence is needed to fully establish the canal-irrigation system during the Harappan times, there is little doubt that the Dholavirans knew how to dam streamlets, take out channels from the dams and use the water as needed (Fig. 4.41). Whether this water was also used for field-irrigation is not yet clear. However, damming streamlets and utilizing their water are not uncommon in the rural areas even nowadays.

Fig. 4.39 Dholavira: A stone-lined well in the Castle. The flat slab of the trough (top left) bears abrasion marks left by the ropes that constantly rubbed against it in the process of drawing water. Mature Harappan

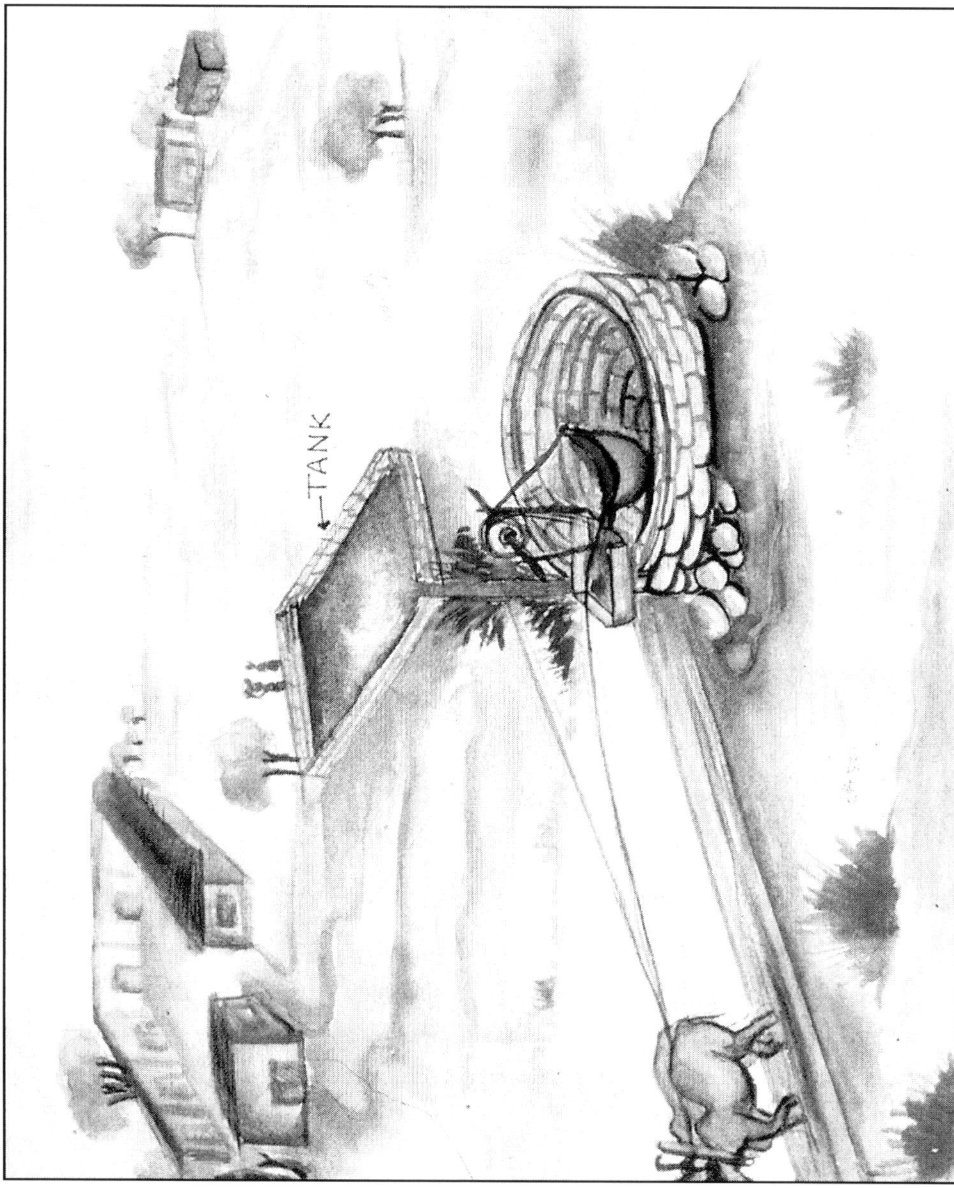

4.40 Dholavira: A sketch to illustrate how water was drawn from the well (Fig. 4.39). This very method was in use in northern India prior to the recent introduction of electrically operated tube-wells

Fig. 4.41 Dholavira: A sketch to illustrate how an adjacent streamlet was dammed and water was brought to a reservoir during the Mature Harappan times

(VI) TRANSPORT, ON LAND AND WATER

Bullock carts as a means of land-transport are known right from the Early Harappan times. These seem to have been made of wood, but because of the perishable nature of the material actual examples have not been found. Nevertheless, the probable shape of these vehicles seems to be suggested by the models of their frames and wheels, both in terracotta. Fig. 4.42 shows a reconstruction of the bullock cart, based on the parts in terracotta. The long pole has been inserted in the hole occurring on the frontal side of the frame. However, what is of greater interest is the fact that more or similar is the configuration of the bullock carts used in the villages even today. In fact, Marshall published in his report on Mohenjo-daro (1931: Vol. III, pl. CLIV, 11) the photographs of a modern Sindhi cart which compares well with the ancient examples. In this context, it needs to be added that the wheels were both solid and spoked (cf. Figs. 3.28-30, above).

But much more exciting has been the discovery of the **cart-tracks** at Harappa (Wheeler 1947: pl.XXXVB, here Fig. 4.43). These were encountered just above the natural soil in the area later used by the Cemetery H people for burying their dead. Since this cemetery succeeded Mature Harappan, the high antiquity of the cart-tracks is duly established. These may have belonged to the Harappan or even Early Harappan times. Six ruts were identified, covering an overall width of about 4 m, while the distance between each pair of corresponding ruts was about 1.08 m. Yet another surprising part of the story is that the **gauge of the ancient carts, as deduced from these ruts, is similar to that of the modern Sindhi carts. And if the Harappa evidence was not enough, let it be added that similar ruts have also been found at Banawali**.

The chariot was another type of vehicle used by the Harappans as indicated by a model in copper, found at Harappa (Vats 1940: Vol. II, pl. CXXV, 35). It is interesting to note that this form survives in the *ekka* used in eastern Uttar Pradesh and Bihar even today, though because of motorized transport it is fast dying out.

From land transport we may move on to that on water. A seal from Mohenjo-daro depicts a boat with a central cabin (Fig. 4.44). Commenting on it, Mackay (1938: Vol. I, p.341) states: 'The absence of a mast suggests that this boat was used only for river work, as are some of the wooden boats on

the Indus at the present day; though the modern boats have a less acutely upturned prow and stern, they usually have a similar cabin-like erection in the middle, sometimes constructed of wood and sometimes of reeds.' Kenoyer (1998: Fig. 5.19) has published a photograph of a boat (here Fig. 4.45) which is almost similar to that from Mohenjo-daro.

Lothal in Gujarat, not far from the Gulf of Khambhat and connected to it by a system of channels, has, as stated earlier, given to us the earliest dockyard known to humanity. It has also yielded some terracotta models of boats. Of these, one has holes indicating the positions where poles for the mast and sail were fixed. Such boats are now used for coastal sea-voyages. Discussing

Top left : Fig. 4.42 Kalibangan: Reconstruction of a bullock-cart, on the basis of terracotta samples of frames and wheels. Mature Harappan

Bottom left : Fig. 4.43 Harappa: Early cart-tracks beneath Cemetery H

Fig. 4.44 Mohenjo-daro: Impression of a seal, depicting a boat with a cabin. Mature Harappan

Fig. 4.45 A modern boat with a cabin, on the Indus in Pakistan

the other types, Rao (1979: Vol I, p.132) says: 'There is yet another model which is very narrow but long, almost similar to the catamarans of South India used mostly as fishing boats near the coast.'

(VII) CRAFTS

To meet the needs of the people, all kinds of objects are prepared and each variety requires special skill and thus come into being the crafts and craftsmen. The same was the case during the Harappan times. Hence, there were the potters, metal-smiths, wood-carvers, textile-workers, lapidaries, seal-cutters and so on. While some of these crafts are of a routine nature such as pottery-making, some others are highly specialized, like seal-cutting. Here we propose to highlight some of the more noteworthy Harappan crafts which are still continuing.

Fig. 4.46 Lothal: Kiln for bead-making. Mature Harappan

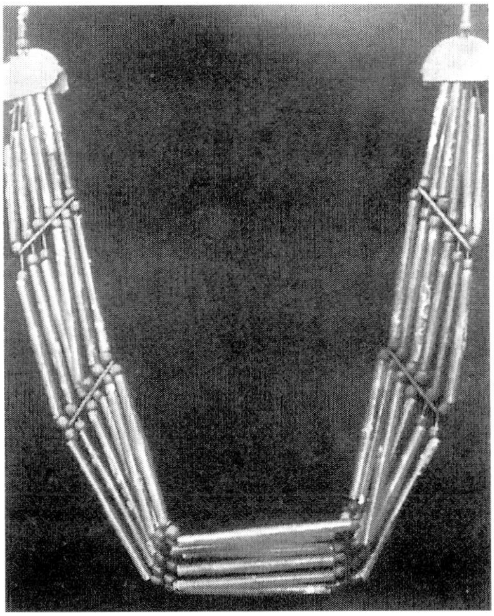

The production of objects in various metals, such as copper, silver and gold, was a specialized craft with the Harappans. It involved the procurement of the raw material from far off places since the plains around the sites did not yield the same. In the case of copper, the ore was melted, purified and turned into ingots which were then made available to the specialized craftsmen to produce a variety of objects, ranging from ordinary pins to hefty cooking utensils.

Left : Fig. 4.47 Mohenjo-daro: Belt or necklace of carnelian beads. Mature Harappan
Bottom : Fig. 4.48 A stage in the bead-making process, Gujarat

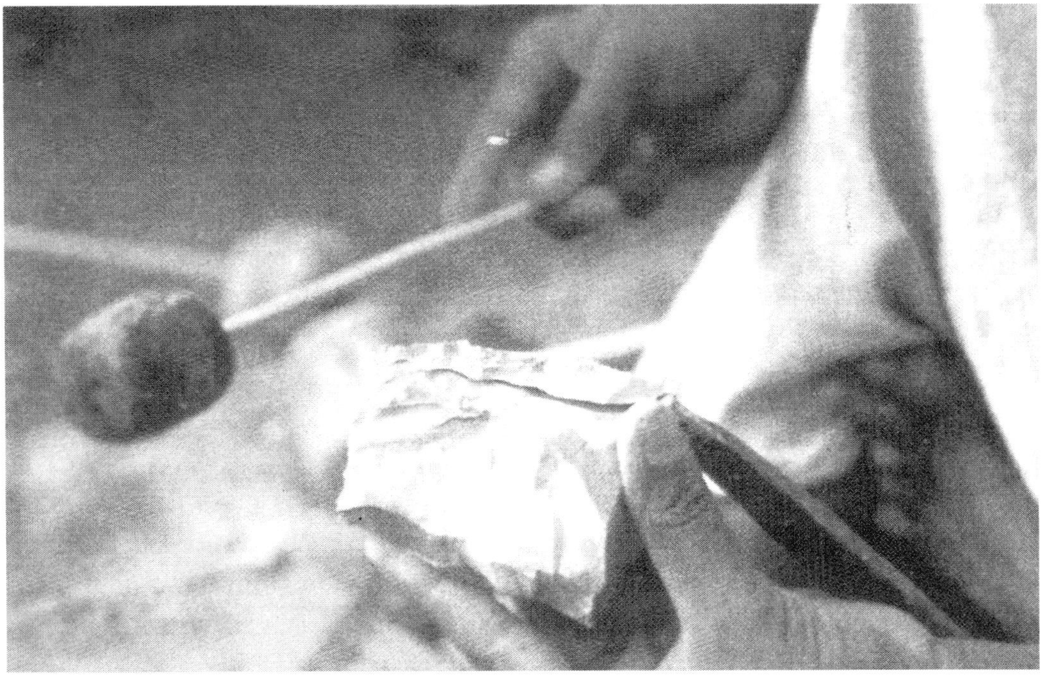

Fig. 4.49 Kalibangan: Terracotta model of a cot, with the bedspread shown in black-and-white design. Early Harappan

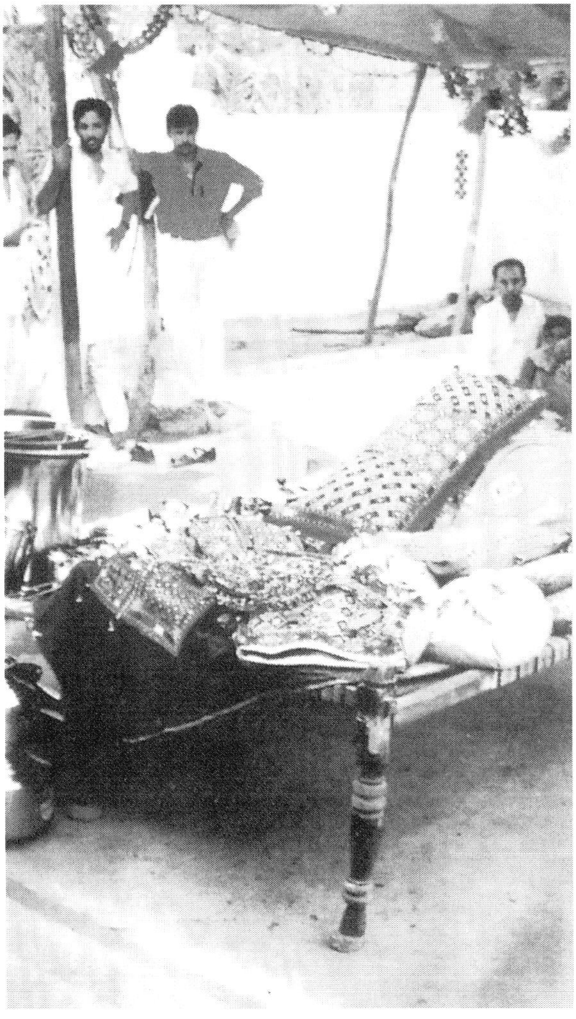

Fig. 4.50 Example of a modern cot, loaded with clothes including printed bedspreads

All sorts of techniques appear to have been known to the Harappans, such as 'sinking', 'raising', 'cold-working', 'annealing', 'lapping', 'closed casting' and last but not least *cire perdu*. It is interesting to note that all these techniques, including that of *cire perdu*, are in use even today.

Equally interesting is the case of lapidary, for which the Harappans were well known, even in Western and Central Asia, whereto a whole lot of beads, particularly the etched carnelian ones, were exported. Amongst others, Lothal in Gujarat was one of the centres where beads of semi-precious stones, including carnelian, were produced during the Harappan times. (Fig. 4.46 shows a bead-making kiln from Lothal.) But what is really remarkable is that the industry is still flourishing in that part of the country and the trade goes on as ever. (While Fig. 4.47 shows a necklace of carmelian leads from the Mature Harappan levels of Mohenjo-daro, Fig. 4.48 shows a stage in the process of bead-making today.)

In the hot and humid climate of India, organic materials like wood and textile are rarely preserved and therefore it is difficult to ascertain what kind of objects were manufactured in these media. Nonetheless, a glimpse of them can be had through another source, viz. from their representation in the terracotta medium, which does withstand time. Thus, what a Harappan cot (Hindi *chārapāī*) looked like can be easily made out from its copy in terracotta. Most of the Harappan sites have yielded its examples, but here we illustrate only one, viz. that from the Early Harappan levels of Kalibangan. In it (Fig. 4.49) not only is the shape of the cot indicated, which is similar to that of the present-day cots used in the region, but some interesting additional information is also provided (Madhu Bala 1997). The specimen bears a design painted in black and white colours and it is most likely that the craftsman-cum-artist wanted to show the design on the bedspread. Bedspreads (*darīs*) with more or less similar designs may be bought in the rural markets of Rajasthan, Haryana and Panjab. Fig. 4.50 shows a modern cot on which are lying about lots of things including printed bedspreads.

(VIII) AND FOLK TALES TOO

It is most unbelievable, yet it seems to be true, that some of our folk tales had their origin during the Harappan times. Whether the Harappan grandmothers too narrated these tales to their grandchildren at bedtime, as do their modern counterparts, is anybody's guess. The evidence regarding these tales comes from painted scenes on pottery, discovered in the Mature Harappan levels at Lothal.

Fig. 4.51 shows a small red ware vase with a scene painted in black colour, the details of which are reproduced in the panel below it. The main actors

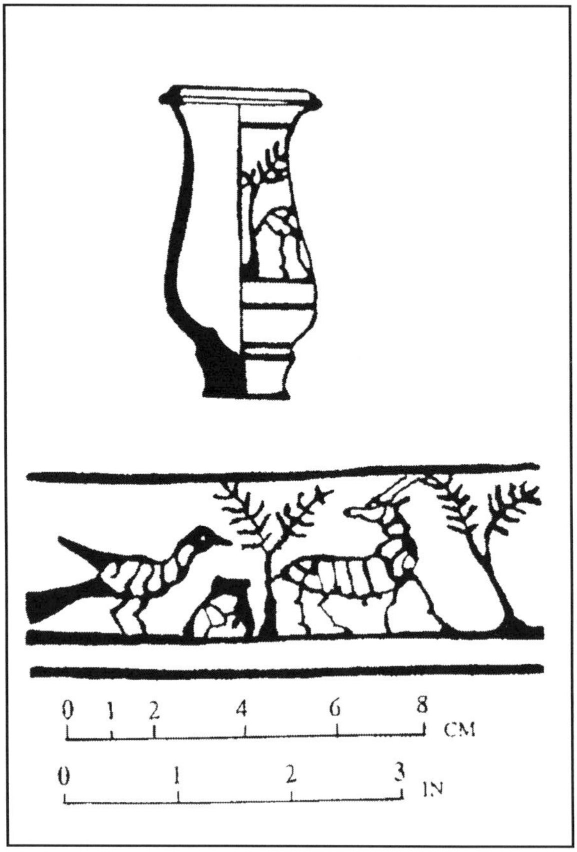

Fig. 4.51 Lothal: A vase, the painting on which appears to narrate the story of 'The Thirsty Crow'. Mature Harappan

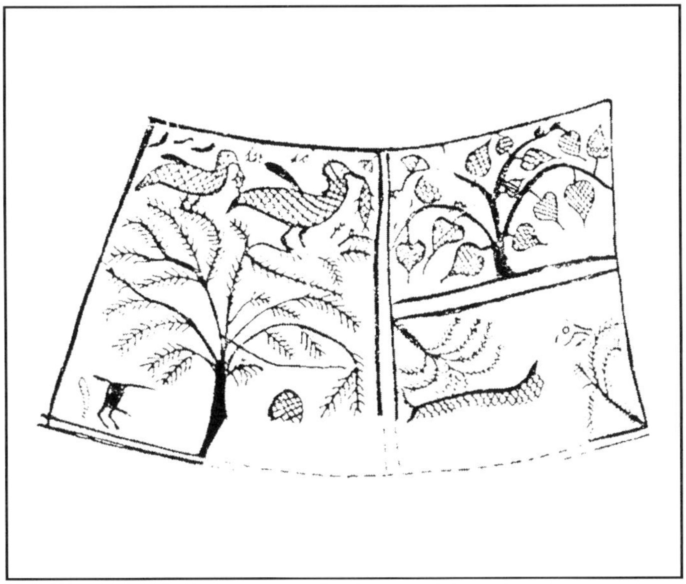

Fig. 4.52 Lothal: Painting on another jar seems to narrate the story of 'The Cunning Fox'. Mature Harappan

are a deer and a crow and the story revolves around the pitcher which is in between them. The scene also depicts two trees, one in front of the deer and the other between the deer and the pitcher, but these have no role in the story. The outstretched front right leg of the deer indicates that the animal is about to go away. However, his neck is turned backwards and the eyes are wide open, which suggest that he is looking with some kind of amazement at the crow. The crow's beak is right above the pitcher, indicating that it has just taken it out of the latter. The contents of the pitcher cannot be easily made out since these are within it. Nevertheless one can see some roundish object and a couple of lines. The roundish object perhaps represents a pebble or something like that. All told, the scene seems to narrate the story of 'The Thirsty Crow'. According to this story, there was water in a pitcher and a thirsty deer wanted to drink it. The water was at a low level and the deer could not manage to push his head deep enough into the pitcher to reach the water-level, particularly because of his horns. Disappointed, as he was about to walk away, he noticed a crow near the pitcher. The crow too was thirsty. But he was intelligent enough to find a way out. He picked up and dropped some pebbles into the pitcher, as a result of which the water-level rose up and he quenched his thirst.

The other scene seems to narrate the story of 'A Cunning Fox' (Fig. 4.52). This painted jar also comes from the Harappan levels of Lothal. While the other panels depict geometric or floral designs, there is one which portrays the scene under reference. It shows a tree on which two birds are perched.

Each one holds a fish in its beak. The birds as well as the fish are cross-hatched. The bottom right part of the panel is unfortunately broken. Nevertheless, one can see a cross-hatched object. At the bottom left there is an animal, portrayed in solid colour. From the way the tail is depicted it seems that a fox-like animal was meant. Close to it is a small hatched object. Altogether, the story that seems to have been narrated goes as follows. There was a fox that saw some birds sitting on a tree with some food in their mouth. The fox wanted to snatch away the food from the birds. But how to do it? An idea struck the mind of the fox. She thought that she should tell the birds that they were very good singers and request them to give a song. The fox did accordingly. The birds, simpletons as they were, got elated by the praise and started singing. As they opened their mouths, the morsel of food dropped down and the cunning fox ran away with it. In the scene depicted on the pot, the food in the mouths of the birds is shown in the form of fish. The opening of the mouth by the birds and the falling of the fish from their beaks could not be shown simultaneously, unless the artist had drawn another panel to continue the second part of the story. However, the depiction of the fox a little away on the left and the presence nearby of a fish-like hatched object meet the needs of the story. Should we not give credit to the Harappan artist of the third millennium BC to have given us the essentials of the story?

(IX) RELIGION

Religion is an aspect of life which is deeply ingrained in human psyche, even though some people will tend to deny it. While in some cases it may be a genuine enquiry about their own inner being or a search for the phenomenon known as God that draws them towards 'religion' (from Latin *religio-onis* 'obligation, bond, reverence'), in most cases it is a kind of fear of the 'unknown'. When the latter category of people find that not all goes on well with them, they begin to deduce that there is some 'force' beyond them which interferes with their destiny and they take to certain outward practices to propitiate this unknown force. Thus, religion has two aspects, which may be called metaphysical/philosophical and physical/ritualistic. Both these aspects tend to continue generation after generation, of course with evolutionary/devolutionary changes from time to time. However, a fundamental change can take place in the religious beliefs and practices of the people if a new religion is thrust upon them either on the point of the sword or under economic

Fig. 4.53 Mohenjo-daro: Impression of a seal depicting a seated figure surrounded by animals, believed to be Śiva in his aspect of Paśupati (Lord of animals). Mature Harappan

pressures. Anyway, we shall try here to analyze which aspects of the Harappan religion have survived the ages.

As just stated, there are two facets of religion, one theoretical or philosophical and the other practical or ritualistic. The former is carried down either by word of mouth or through written religious texts, whereas the latter leaves material evidence behind for its identification. The Harappans have not left any long texts for us to interpret and even if they had, right now we would not have been able to make any sense out of them, since so far we have miserably failed in decoding the Harappan script. (With due respect to the scores of scholars who claim to have deciphered the script, it has got to be politely but categorically stated that none of them has hit the mark.) We have, therefore, to remain deprived of an insight into the Harappan religious philosophy. However, we can try to reconstruct their beliefs and practices from whatever remains they have left behind.

We may perhaps begin with the oft-quoted seal from Mohenjo-daro which depicts a human figure, seated in a yogic posture, with a number of animals surrounding him (Fig. 4.53). Marshall suggested that the figure might represent Śiva in the form of *Paśupati* (Lord of Animals). He even went to the extent of thinking that, since the figure seems to have three faces, it may be a forerunner of the later-day *Trimūrti* concept (Marshall 1931: Vol. I, 52-55). Most

scholars have accepted the idea of Marshall and it is now generally held that Śaivism, in some incipient form, may have been there during the Harappan times.

There is another kind of evidence which seems to affirm the foregoing hypothesis about the presence of Śaivism in the third millennium BC. Marshall identified certain stone objects found in the excavations at Mohenjo-daro as *liṅga*s and *yoni*s (Marshall 1931: Vol. I, pl. XIV, 2 and 4; and 6 and 8 respectively). However, not all scholars were fully convinced of Marshall's identification and a kind of doubt lingered on in this regard. The excavations at Kalibangan have since removed the doubt. For here has been found a terracotta specimen which is clearly identifiable as *liṅga*-cum-*yoni* (Fig. 4.54), something we come across

Top left : Fig. 4.54 Kalibangan: Terracotta *liṅga*-cum-*yoni*. Mature Harappan

Bottom left : Fig. 4.55 Śiva *liṅga* and *yoni* in a modern temple. From the overhead pitcher water-drops keep on dripping on the *liṅga*

Fig. 4.56 Harappa: Terracotta tablet, depicting the Śiva-like seated figure (right) and a person attempting to kill a buffalo, perhaps as a sacrifice. Mature Harappan

so commonly in the Śaivite temples today (Fig. 4.55).

At this point attention may also be drawn to a terracotta plano-convex tablet found recently at Harappa (Kenoyer 1998: fig. 6.24b; here Fig. 4.56). On it a seated figure is shown on the right, which, though not as elaborately drawn as that on the seal illustrated in Fig. 4.53, seems to represent the same deity, as suggested by the special yogic posture as well as the head-dress. As stated earlier, it has been taken to be that of Śiva. On the left is depicted a buffalo with a man in the front. The man presses the head of the animal with his right foot, holds one of the animal's horns with his left hand and pierces the back of the animal with a spear held in his right hand. The scene may well be called as that of *mahiṣa-mardana,* i.e. sacrificing a buffalo before Śiva. It is not unlikely that the later-day concept of Mahiṣamardinī, in which the consort of Śiva herself kills the animal-demon, may have emerged from it, though this will remain a conjecture unless we come across evidence from intervening periods.

Sacrificing animals on special religious occasions is common enough these days, particularly in rural India. The animal is tied to a rope and taken to

Fig. 4.57 Kalibangan: Obverse and reverse of a terracotta 'cake'. On one side is shown a horned deity and on the other an animal pulled by a man with a rope. Mature Harappan

the place of sacrifice. A glimpse into this practice during the Harappan times is given by an engraved terracotta 'cake' found at Kalibangan (Fig. 4.57). (For no special reason has this nomenclature been given to such triangular or spheroid terracotta objects, but is retained in archaeological literature.) The cake is broken hence the full scene is not available. Nevertheless, on one side may be seen an animal tied with a rope and pulled by a man. On the other side is a figure which, on the basis of the special head-dress, appears to be a deity. The overall interpretation, putting the portrayal on the two sides together, would obviously be that the animal is being taken by the man for sacrifice before a deity. That animal-sacrifice was actually practised by the Harappans is clearly proved by the discovery at Kalibangan of a brick-lined sacrificial pit. In it have been found antlers and bovine bones (Fig. 4.58).

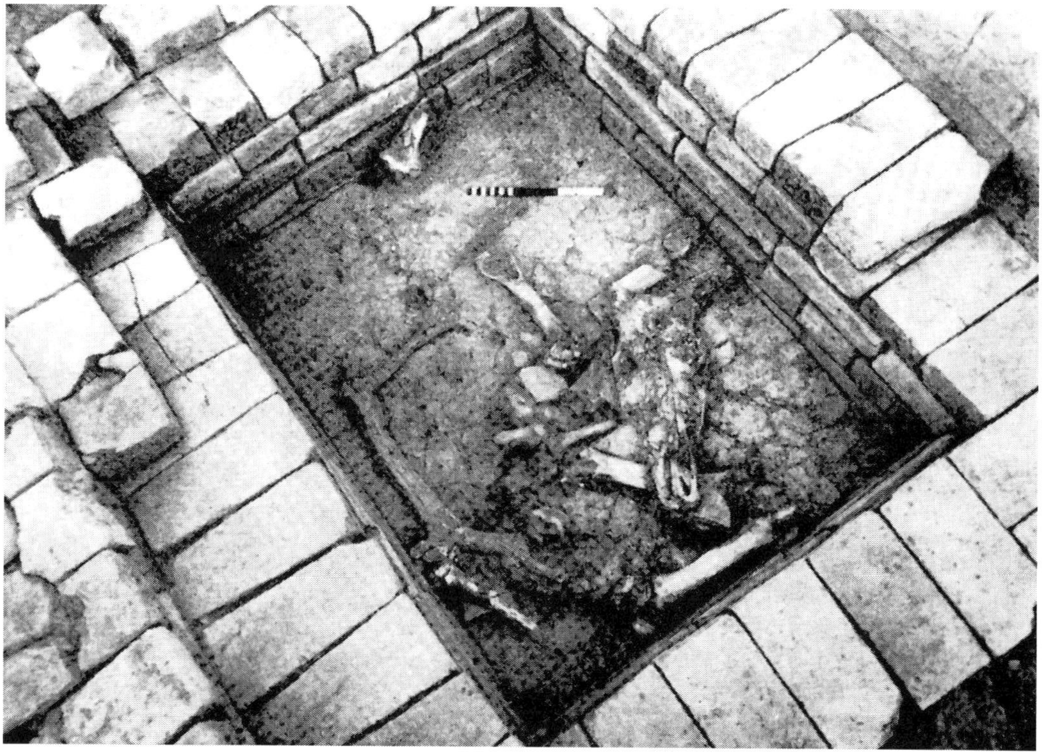

Fig. 4.58 Kalibangan: This brick-lined sacrificial pit, containing bovine bones and antlers, was discovered on a platform in the southern half of the Citadel. Mature Harappan

Rituals associated with fire are quite common in Hindu religion. These are there in many Vedic sacrifices (*yajñas*). Quite often *havana* is performed in Hindu households and for that fire is lit in a *havana-kuṇḍa*. Some kind of fire ritual was also practised during the Harappan times and ample evidence in this regard has been obtained from Kalibangan, Banawali, Rakhigarhi and Lothal. Here we shall discuss in some detail the data from Kalibangan.

It appears that in the houses in the Lower Town one of the rooms was specially earmarked for rituals associated with fire. The 'fire-altars' (called so in the absence of a better name, but not to be confused with the Parsi fire-altars) were roughly rectangular on plan, measuring about a metre in length and half that in width (Fig. 4.59). These were dug into the ground usually to a depth of 25-30 cm and plastered on the interior with clay. Roughly in the

Fig. 4.59 Kalibangan: A 'fire-altar' in a house in the Lower Town. Mature Harappan

Fig. 4.60 Kalibangan: A row of seven 'fire-altars' discovered on a platform in the southern half of the Citadel. Mature Harappan

Fig. 4.61 Mohenjo-daro: Impression of a seal, showing in the upper register a deity within an enclosure of pipal branches, a kneeling devotee and an animal perhaps brought in for sacrifice. In the lower register there are seven human figures marching in a row. Mature Harappan

central part there stood a cylindrical or faceted stele of clay, sometimes even fired. It measured about 15 cm across and had a height of about 30-40 cm. Around it there lay terracotta 'cakes', usually circular-biconvex in shape. It seems likely that these were placed there as some kind of offering. Besides these, the altar contained ash and charcoal, signifying the use of fire in the ritual.

While the foregoing was the situation in the houses in the general habitation area, the Citadel presented a different picture. In its southern half there were several mud-brick platforms, each carrying some significant structural or ritual remains. The brick-lined pit associated with animal-sacrifice, referred to earlier, was found on one of these platforms. On another platform there was a series of contiguous altars (Fig. 4.60). Although a subsequent drain destroyed some of the evidence, one can nonetheless make out that their total number was seven—whatever may have been the significance of that number. Within the altars one may also see here and there the remains of the stele and 'cakes'. In front of the altars is seen the lower half of an earthen jar, placed in a pit. It was full of ash and charcoal, indicating that fire was kept ready in it for the ritual. Another interesting feature noted was that behind the altars there was a wall running north-south. Thus, anybody who used these altars had to face the east. Close to the altars there was a well with an attached bathing pavement (not appearing in this photograph). It would appear that the worshippers had to have a bath before performing the ritual. Many of the foregoing observances, such as facing the east or having a bath, are still observed by Hindus when they perform *yajña* or *havana*.

Tree-worship is yet another feature that seems to have come down from the Harappan times. For example, we see these days people worshipping the pipal tree (*ficus religiosa*), often under the belief that some deity resides in it. In a like manner, the Harappan belief seems to be highlighted by a seal (Fig. 4.61) which shows, in the upper register, a deity standing within a U-shaped enclosure made of the branches of pipal tree. Close to it is a kneeling devotee with an animal behind him, presumably meant for offering. In the lower register there are seven human figures, evidently associated with the ritual.

Certain symbols too have come down from the Harappan days, amongst which particular mention may be made of the svastika (Fig. 4.62). What significance was attached to it by the Harappans it is difficult to guess, but today it is regarded as a symbol of good luck. It is used on religious occasions and often painted by Hindus on either side of the entrance of their house, specially in the rural areas (Fig. 4.63).

Top left : Fig. 4.62 Mohenjo-daro: The svastika motif engraved on a seal. Mature Harappan

Bottom left : Fig. 4.63 Entrance to a Hindu house, painted with svastika symbol on either side

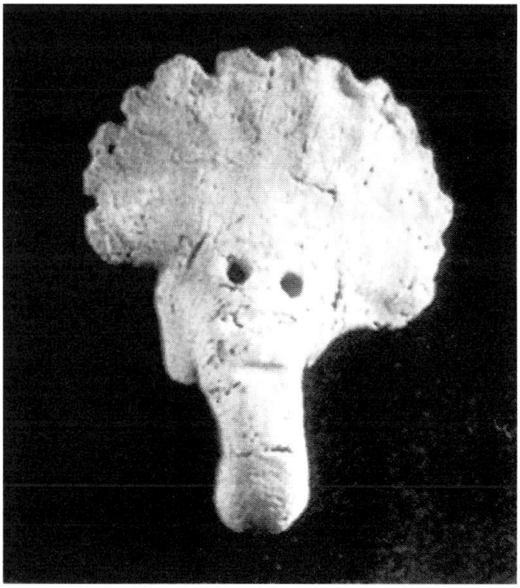

Fig. 4.64a Harappa: The head and trunk of a terracotta elephant, painted. Mature Harappan

Fig. 4.64b Elephants with painted forehead and trunk

Top : Fig. 4.65 The President of India, Shri K.R. Narayanan (extreme left), being greeted with *namaste* by the Prime Minister, Shri Atal Bihari Vajpayee (extreme right), and other dignitaries on the eve of the President's departure on a foreign tour

Bottom right : Fig. 4.66 Harappa: A terracotta figurine greeting with *namaste*. Mature Harappan

On the occasion of religious processions, it is customary to decorate elephants, particularly their forehead and trunk, with paints (cf. Fig. 4.64b). It is interesting to note that the practice of painting elephants' forehead and trunk goes back to the Harappan times (Fig. 4.64a).

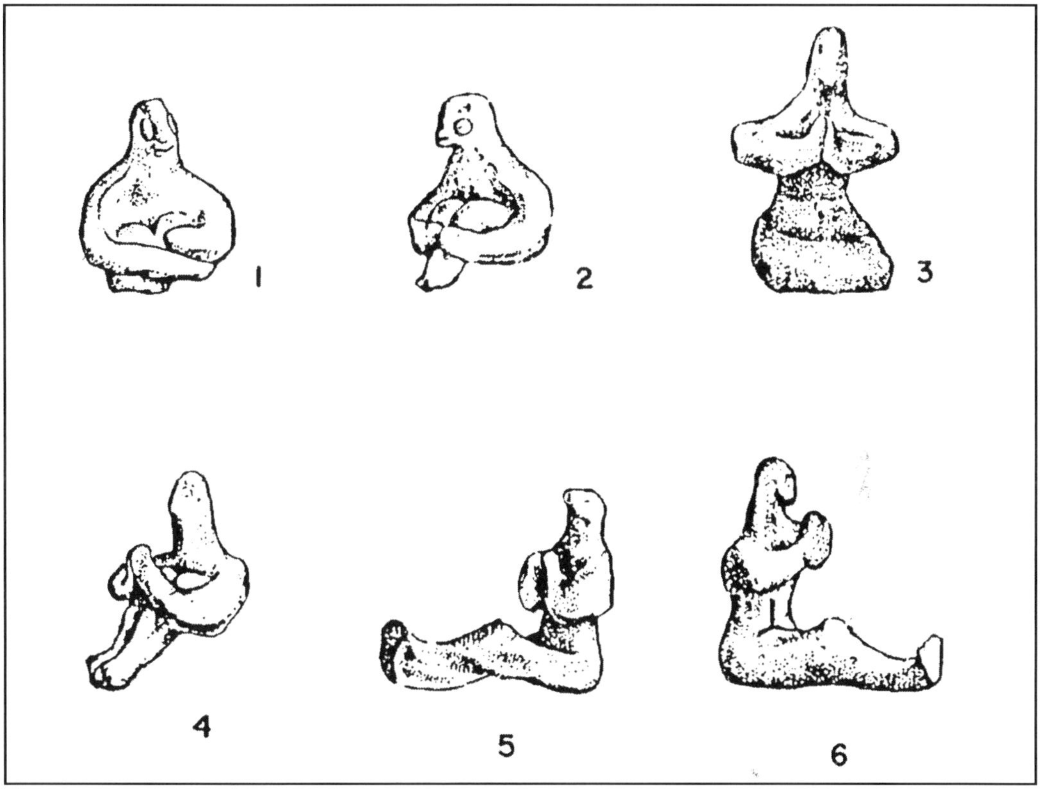

4.67 Terracotta figurines in Yogic *āsana*s: 1-4, from Harappa; 5-6, from Mohenjo-daro. Mature Harappan

One does not know if one should classify the Hindu way of greeting, viz. the *Namaste* (Fig. 4.65), merely as a social observance or a religious practice. This query arises since the greeting implies obeisance to (the divinity within) the person so greeted. Anyway, the point of interest here is that this form has come down to us from the Harappan times, as indicated by the terracotta figurines of that period (Fig. 4.66).

This takes us to another aspect of Harappan life, namely the practice of yogic *āsana*s. The terracotta figurines shown in Fig. 4.67 clearly indicate that the Harappans practised *āsanas*. Standing midway between the present and the Harappan times, Patañjali deals with the various aspects of yoga in his treatise, the *Yogasūtra*. It speaks of eight steps in the complete practice of yoga,

Fig. 4.68 Mohenjo-daro: Limestone statue of a 'priest'. The introvert eyes are indicative of *dhyāna mudrā* (meditative pose). Mature Harappan

viz. *yama, niyama, āsana, prāṇāyāma, pratyāhāra, dhāraṇā, dhyāna* and *samādhi*. While we have just seen the evidence of the *āsana*s during the Harappan times, there is equally good indication of *dhyāna*. And here we shall draw attention to the limestone statue of the priest from Mohenjo-daro (Fig. 4.68). The eyes are introvert, which is what happens in the *dhyāna*-stage (meditation). While dealing with the practice of yoga, the *Bhagvadgītā* uses the term '*samprekṣya nāsikāgram*' which has been taken by the commentators to mean fixing the gaze on either the 'tip' or 'root' of the nose. Elsewhere the same text uses the expression '*bhruvor-madhye*', suggesting that the gaze should be fixed between the eyebrows. This is also the place of the *ājñā-chakra*, the centre where the yogi has all extrasensory perceptions. In Western mystic literature this location is known as 'the place of Christ-consciousness'. Without being too particular about these nuances, it is pretty clear that the above-mentioned terracotta figurines and the limestone priest do point to the practice of yoga by the Harappans.

(X) SOCIAL HIERARCHY

Before closing this chapter on Harappan legacy, we would like to have a look at the social hierarchy during the Harappan times and examine if it has in any way come down to us. However, in ascertaining the situation during the Harappan days we are greatly handicapped by our inability to decipher the Harappan script. Were we able to read the inscriptions on the various Harappan objects, such as seals, sealings, pots, ivory and metal objects, etc., we would have possibly come across the names of some professions, or of guilds engaged in trade, or even surnames. That being not the case, we have to look to another kind of evidence for reconstructing the social hierarchy amongst the Harappans.

While most of the Harappan sites, be it Harappa itself or Mohenjo-daro or Lothal or Kalibangan, throw valuable light on the social divisions amongst the Harappan people, we shall take the last-named site as a case study. In doing so there is bound to be some repetition of what has been stated earlier, but that is inevitable since the very basis of the conclusions that follow has got to be put in the right perspective. Thus, as mentioned in chapter III, there were two major parts of the settlement at Kalibangan, the 'Citadel' on the west and the 'Lower Town' on the east, each being separately fortified (see Fig. 3.10). Again, the Citadel itself had two divisions, one on the north and the other on the south, separated by a partition wall. In the southern part of the Citadel there were many platforms over which stood some significant structures. In the sub-section on religion, we referred to the two extant complexes, viz. the 'fire-altars' and a sacrificial pit (respectively Figs. 4.60 and 58). (Since the other platforms have been badly eroded it was not possible to identify the structures thereon.) In contrast, the northern part of the Citadel had residential buildings and it has been surmised that in this part there lived the priests who participated in as well as supervised the various rituals that were performed on the platforms in the southern part. All this evidence shows that there was a priestly class in the Harappan society. In fact, it reminds us also of the limestone bust of the priest, found at Mohenjo-daro (Fig. 4.68).

In the Lower Town there were no platforms nor any special structural complexes. The settlement within the fortified area was divided into blocks by streets running north-south and east-west (see Figs. 3.10, 12 and 13). Each block comprised a few houses and each house usually had five to six living rooms, laid along three sides of a large courtyard. On the fourth side there was a wide entrance which allowed bullock-carts and domestic animals to freely get in. Within the courtyard there were troughs to hold fodder and water for the animals. One of the rooms was generally used for storage of grains, as indicated by the presence in it of storage jars. The overall setting of such houses indicates that herein lived the agriculturists. In some other houses were found a few seals as well, suggesting that the occupants also carried on trade. Thus, the Lower Town was the area wherein lived an agriculturist-cum-merchant community.

South of the Citadel there was an open (i.e. unfortified) area (see Fig. 3.10). The houses here were much smaller than those in the Lower Town, nor were there any special buildings. Though the excavation in this part was not very extensive, at one location a large amount of broken pottery and ash were encountered, suggesting that somewhere in the neighbourhood may have lived the community of potters. The smallness of the houses combined with this pottery evidence would suggest that in this unfortified part of Kalibangan there lived the labour class, attending to the needs of those who occupied the Citadel and the Lower Town. In this context one may well recall the working floors and workmen's quarters in the shadow of the Citadel at Harappa (Fig. 4.69).

Let it be added that Kalibangan and Harappa do not stand isolated in having this kind of settlement-pattern. Similar features are also there at Mohenjo-daro, Lothal and Dholavira. These have been discussed in detail in Lal 1997: 230-32, and need not be repeated here. The overall evidence thus clearly indicates that the Harappan society was divided into at least three classes, viz. a priestly class occupying the Citadel, an agriculturist-cum-merchant community living in the Lower Town and a deprived labour class living in small tenements in an area that was never fortified. Here it may also be worth stating that the occurrence of the same type of material in the successive strata of the houses concerned suggests that this kind of occupational division may have persisted generation after generation. That is to say, the occupations may have become hereditary. In such a situation there may have emerged what we have come to know in its fossilized form as 'caste'.

Admittedly, in the absence of documentary evidence it is not possible to know what were the respective designations of these three aforementioned classes during the Harappan times. Also, it is always risky to look at the past with present-day glasses. At the same time, it may not be out of place to refer

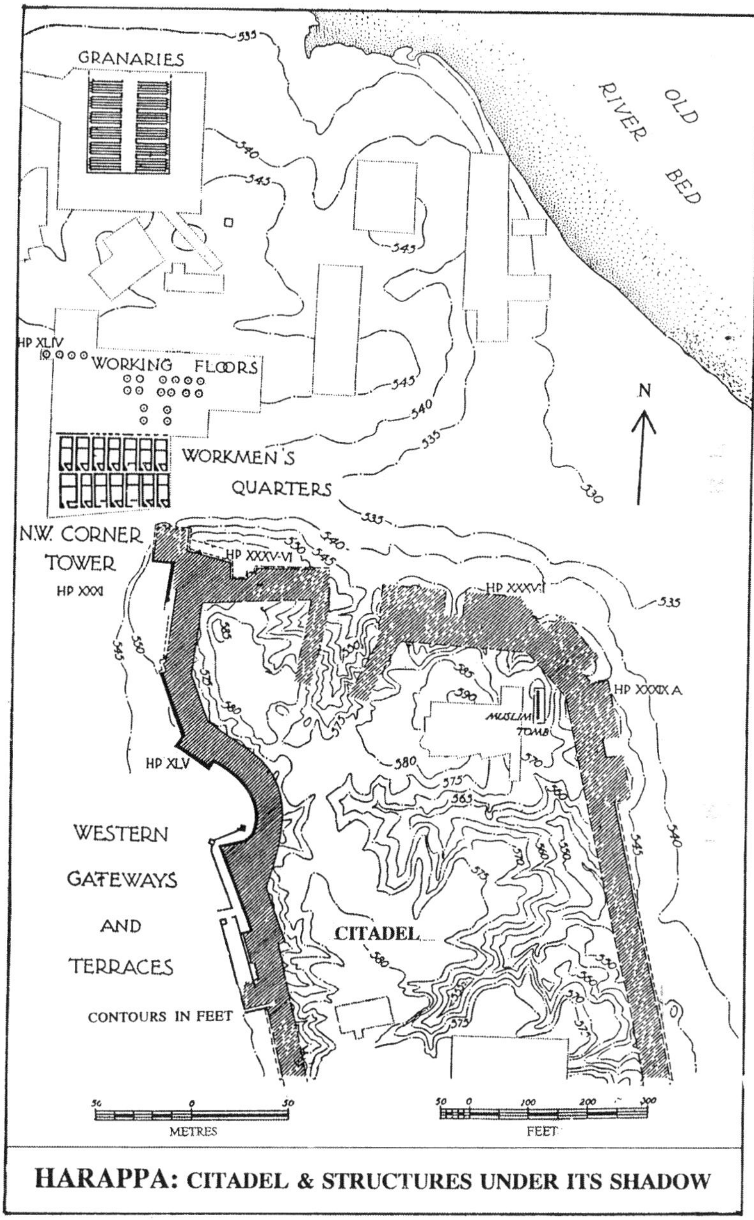

Fig. 4.69 Harappa: Citadel and structures under its shadow

here to the *Bhagvadgītā* which, like the aforementioned *Yogasūtra* of Patañjali, again stands roughly midway between the Harappan times and the present. In it (Chapter IV, Verse 13) Lord Kṛiṣṇa says: '*Chāturvarṇyam mayā sṛiṣṭam guṇa-karma vibhāgaśaḥ,*' i.e. 'I have carved out a fourfold division in the society in accordance with the nature and duties of the people concerned'. This fourfold division consists of the Brāhmaṇas, Kṣatriyas, Vaiṣyas and Śūdras. If the *karma*-(profession-)based Harappan society fossilized in the course of time into a hereditary one, as seems most likely, the Harappan priestly class may have given rise to the Brāhmaṇas, the agriculturist-cum-merchant class to the Vaiṣyas and the labour class to what came to be known as the Śūdras. The warrior class, viz. that of the Kṣatriyas, may have also come into being as a separate entity as and when the need was felt for defence against an enemy in an organized manner.

(XI) THE SCRIPT: ITS CONTINUANCE — A MATTER OF DEBATE

As stated earlier, there are two very divergent views about the language spoken by the Harappans. While some hold that the Harappan language was of the Dravidian group (e.g. Fairservis 1992 and Parpola *et al.* 1969), others believe it to have been Sanskrit (e.g. S.R. Rao 1982, Krishna Rao 1982 and Jha 1996). In fact, one scholar even reads Vedic verses in the inscriptions on the Harappan seals (Richter-Ushanas 1992). This is not the place to discuss the merits or demerits of these claims and it would suffice here to say that none has really hit the mark. (Those interested in the issue may refer to Lal 1970, 1974 and 1983; and Possehl 1996.)

Fig. 4.70 Mohenjo-daro: Writing tablets (*takhtīs*) represented in terracotta. Mature Harappan

Fig. 4.71 Yamuna Nagar: A third-second century BC terracotta plaque. It shows a child pointing out one of the Brāhmī alphabets written on a *takhtī*

However, a question might still be asked, viz. was the Brāhmī script, used by Asoka for his inscriptions all over the country, derived from the Harappan script? There are some scholars who believe it was (e.g. Jha 1996), but the case does not seem to have been duly established. There is little doubt that the signs used in the Harappan script continued much after the end of the Mature Harappan days, into the chalcolithic and megalithic times. More importantly, it is not the mere continuance of some individual signs that is of significance; what is noteworthy is that from a megalithic grave at Sanur has been recovered a pot which bears three signs **in a row**, suggesting that it is as much an inscription as any other in the Harappan context (cf. Lal 1960). This grave is ascribable broadly to the first quarter of the first millennium BC. However, there still remains the problem of bridging a gap of about four

Fig. 4.72 School children writing on wooden *takhtīs*

to five centuries between the Sanur example and the earliest known examples of the Brāhmī script. Besides, of course, there is the more critical task of interconnecting the two morphologically as well as phonologically.

While we must await further research to determine whether or not the Brāhmī script was really derived from the Harappan, there is some interesting evidence from Mohenjo-daro regarding what have been called by Mackay as 'writing-tablets'. There are two rectangular objects in terracotta, one complete, and the other broken, the former measuring 18 × 8 cm. Both have a small rectangular projection at one of the shorter sides and one also has a hole pierced through this projection (Fig. 4.70). Elaborating on these objects, Mackay writes (1938, Vol. I: 430): 'The use of these two objects is as yet uncertain, but I suggest that they were writing-tablets. It would, of course, be very difficult to inscribe anything upon their present very rough surfaces, but these may once have been covered with some smooth preparation that would allow of writing or numbers being washed off when finished with. In shape these objects are exactly like the large wooden writing-boards that are used at the present day by children in the Panjab and elsewhere (Panjabi, *phatti*; Urdu, *tukhti*).' It seems that, like the terracotta toy-carts referred to earlier, these terracotta *takhtīs* were also toys meant to represent their wooden counterparts.

In this context it needs to be stated that quite a few terracotta plaques showing children writing on *takhtīs* have been recovered from sites in northern India, ascribable to the third-second century BC. On some of the plaques even the Brāhmī alphabets may be clearly seen (Fig. 4.71; Yoganand Shastri 1999: 182-84).

Although such *takhtīs* have almost disappeared from the urban schools where paper and pen are used, they may still be seen in schools in some parts of India (Fig. 4.72). As a child, I myself used a wooden *takhtī* of this very shape, the size, however, being much bigger. It also had a hole in the small projected adjunct, through which a thick thread was passed in order to hang it on a nail affixed to a wall, when not in use.

CHAPTER V

IN RETROSPECT

We have now seen that, contrary to the general belief, this great civilization of the Indian subcontinent, which had its roots deep in antiquity, some seven to eight thousand years ago, and its flowering in the third millennium BC, still lives on, not as a fugitive but as a vital organ of our socio-cultural fabric. In contrast, when we look round the world we are surprised by the fact that the Egyptian and Mesopotamian civilizations that flourished alongside this Indian civilization have all disappeared, leaving hardly any trace behind. All this should, and in fact it does, set us thinking: **Why?** The Indian psyche has indeed been pondering over this great cultural phenomenon of 'livingness', and this quest has been very aptly echoed by a great Indian thinker and poet, Allama Iqbal, in the following words:

Yūnān-o-Misra Rūmā sab miṭ gaye jahān se
Ab tak magar hai bāqī nāmo-nishān hamārā
Kuchh bāt hai ki hastī miṭatī nahīn hamārī
Sadiyon rahā hai dushman daur-ī-zamān hamārā

Freely translated, the verse says: Ancient civilizations of Greece, Egypt and Rome have all disappeared from this world, but the elements of our civilization still continue. Although world-events have been inimical to us for centuries, there is **something** in our civilization which has withstood these onslaughts.

What is that 'something', some inherent strength? Doubtless it lies in the liberal character of the Indian civilization, which allows for cross-fertilization with other cultures, **without losing its own identity**. Even Time (*Kāla*), the great devourer, has stood testimony to the fact that the deep foundations of Indian culture could not be shaken either by internal upheavals, howsoever great may have been their magnitude on the Richter scale, or by the infiltrating extra-territorial cultural waves, howsoever super-cyclonic may have been their thrust. We may well recall the philosophy of the greatest man of our times, Mahatma Gandhi: Let me keep my doors and windows open so that fresh air may enter from all directions. Nevertheless, he was firmly seated in his room (the soul). **The soul of India lives on!**

BIBLIOGRAPHY

Akram, M. 1971. *Reconnaissance Soil Survey of Bahawalpur Area*. Lahore: Soil Survey of Pakistan.

Bisht, R.S. 1982. Excavations at Banawali: 1974-77. In G.L. Possehl (ed.), *Harappan Civilization: A Contemporary Perspective*, pp.113-124. New Delhi: Oxford and IBH Publishing Co.

——. 1987. Further Excavation at Banawali: 1983-84. In B.M. Pande and B.D. Chattopadhyaya (eds.), *Archaeology and History: Essays in Memory of Shri A. Ghosh*, Vol. I, pp.135-56. Delhi: Agam Kala Prakashan.

——. 1991. Dholavira: New Horizons of the Indus Civilization. *Puratattva*, 20: 71-82.

——. 1994. Banawali, also Dholavira. In J.P. Joshi and R.S. Bisht, *India and the Indus Civilization*. New Delhi: National Museum Institute.

Caland, W. 1931 (reprinted 1982). *Pañcaviṁśa Brāhmaṇa*. Calcutta: Asiatic Society.

Dales, G.F. 1964. The Mythical Massacre at Mohenjo-daro. *Expedition*, 6(3): 36-43.

Dales, G.F. and J.M. Kenoyer. 1991. Summaries of Five Seasons of Research at Harappa (District Sahiwal, Punjab, Pakistan), 1986-1990. In Richard H. Meadow (ed.). *Harappa Excavations 1986-1990*, pp.185-262. Madison, Wisconsin: Prehistory Press.

Dikshit, K.N. 1982. Hulas and the Late Harappan Complex in Western Uttar Pradesh. In G.L. Possehl (ed.), *Harappan Civilization: A Contemporary Perspective*, pp.339-51. New Delhi: Oxford and IBH Publishing Co.

Fairservis, W.A. 1992. *The Harappan Civilization and its Writing*. New Delhi: Oxford and IBH Publishing Co.

Flam, Louis. 1999. The Prehistoric Indus River System and the Indus Civilization in Sindh. *Man and Environment*, Vol. XXIV, No. 2, pp.35-69

Griffith, R.T.H. 1995 (reprint). *The Hymns of the Ṛigveda*. 2 vols. Delhi: Low Price Publications.

Gupta, S.P. 1996. *The Indus-Sarasvatī Civilization: Origins, Problems and Issues*. Delhi: Pratibha Prakashan.

Habib, Irfan and Faiz Habib. 1991-92. The Historical Geography of India, 1800-800 B.C. *Proceedings, Indian History Congress: 52nd Session*, pp.72-97.

Hemphill, B.E., J.R. Lukacs and K.A.R. Kennedy. 1991. Biological Adaptations and Affinities of Bronze Age Harappans. In R.H. Meadow (ed.), *Harappa Excavations 1986-1990*, pp.137-82. Madison, Wisconsin: Prehistory Press.

Jarrige, J.-F. and Monique Lechevallier: 1979. Excavations at Mehrgarh, Baluchistan: Their Significance in the Prehistorical context of the Indo-Pakistani Borderlands. *South Asian Archaeology 1977*, pp.463-535.

——. *et al.* (in press), *Excavations at Mehrgarh-Nausharo, 16th to 20th Seasons (1990-94)*. Report submitted to Director Genreal of Archaeology and Museums, Government of Pakistan (unpublished, but privately circulated).

Jha, N. 1996. *Vedic Glossary on Indus Seals*. Varanasi: Ganga Kaveri Publishing House.

Jones, William. 1788. The Third Anniversary Discourse. *Asiatick Researches*, Vol. I, pp.415-31.

Joshi, J.P., 1990. *Excavation at Surkotada 1971-72 and Exploration in Kutch*. New Delhi: Archaeological Survey of India.

——. 1993. *Excavation at Bhagwanpura*, 1975-76. New Delhi: Archaeological Survey of India.

Joshi, J.P., Madhu Bala and Jassu Ram. 1984. The Indus Civilization: A Reconsideration on the Basis of Distribution Maps. In B.B. Lal, S.P. Gupta and Shashi Asthana (eds.), *Frontiers of the Indus Civilization*, pp.511-30. New Delhi: Books and Books.

Kenoyer, Jonathan Mark. 1998. *Ancient Cities of the Indus Civilization*. Karachi: Oxford University Press and American Institute of Pakistan Studies.

Khatri, J.S. and M. Acharya. 1995. Kunal: A New Indus-Saraswati Site. *Puratattva*, 25: 84-86.

Krishna Rao, M.V.N. 1982. *Indus Script Deciphered*. Delhi: Agam Kala Prakashan.

Lal, B.B. 1949. Śiśupālgarh 1948: An Early Historical Fort in Eastern India. *Ancient India*, No. 5: 62-105.

——. 1954 & 1955. Excavation at Hastināpura and other Explorations in the Upper Gaṅgā and Sutlej Basins 1950-52. *Ancient India*, Nos. 10 & 11: 4-151.

——. 1960. From the Megalithic to the Harappan: Tracing Back the Graffiti on the Pottery. *Ancient India*, No. 16: 4-24.

——. 1970. Some Observations on Harappan Script. In L. Chandra *et al.* (eds.), *India's Contribution to World Thought and Culture*, pp.189-202. Madras.

——. 1970-71. Perhaps the Earliest Ploughed Field so far Excavated Anywhere in the World. *Puratattva*, 4: 1-3.

Lal, B.B. 1974. *Has the Indus Script been Deciphered? An Assessment of Two Latest Claims.* Shimla: Indian Institute of Advanced Study.

——. 1983. Reading the Indus Script. *Indian and Foreign Review*, 20 (13): 33-36.

——. 1984. The Earliest Datable Earthquake in India. *Science Age* (October 1984), pp.8-9. Bombay: Nehru Centre.

——. 1991. Planned Cooperation between Archaeologists and Scholars of Ancient Literature–A Crying Need. *Man and Environment*, Vol. XVI, No. 1: 5-21.

——. 1992. Antecedents of the signs used in the Indus Script: A discussion. In G. L. Possehl (ed.), *South Asian Archaeology Studies*, pp.45-55. New Delhi: Oxford and IBH Publishing Co.

——. 1997. *The Earliest Civilization of South Asia.* New Delhi: Aryan Books International.

——. 1998. *India 1947-1997: New Light on the Indus Civilization.* New Delhi: Aryan Books International.

Mackay, E.J.H. 1938. *Further Excavations at Mohenjo-daro.* 2 vols. Delhi: Government of India.

Madhu Bala. 1997. Some Unique Antiquities and Pottery from Kalibangan. In J.P. Joshi (ed.), *Facets of Indian Civilization: Recent Perspectives*, Vol. I, pp.103-6. New Delhi: Aryan Books International.

Madhu Bal and Vishnu Kant. 2000. Dhalewan—An Early Harappan Site in Punjab. *Puratattva*, No. 30, pp.42-44.

Marshall, J. 1931. *Mohenjo-daro and the Indus Civilization.* 3 vols. London: Arthur Probsthain.

Misra, V.N. 1994. Indus Civilization and the Ṛigvedic Sarasvatī. In Asko Parpola *et al.* (eds.), *South Asian Archaeology 1993*, pp.511-25. Helsinki.

Mughal, M. Rafique. 1992. The Consequences of River Changes for the Harappan Settlements in Cholistan. *The Eastern Anthropologist*, Vol. 45 (1 & 2), pp.105-16.

——. 1997. *Ancient Cholistan.* Rawalpindi: Ferozsons (Pvt.) Ltd.

Muller, F. Max. 1890, reprint 1979. *Physical Religion.* New Delhi: Asian Educational Services.

Nath, Amarendra. 1997-98. Rakhigarhi: A Harappan Metropolis in the Sarasvati-Drishadvati Divide. *Puratattva*, 28: 39-45.

——. 1998-99. Further Excavations at Rakhigarhi. *Puratattva*, 29: 46-49.

Parpola, A., S. Koskenniemi, S. Parpola and P. Aalto. 1969. *Decipherment of the Proto-Dravidian Inscriptions of the Indus Civilization.* Copenhagen.

Possehl, Gregory L. 1996. *Indus Age: The Writing System.* New Delhi: Oxford & IBH Publishing Co. Pvt. Ltd.

Possehl, Gregory L. 1999. *Indus Age: The Beginnings*. New Delhi: Oxford & IBH Publishing Co. Pvt. Ltd.

Puri, V.M.K. and B.C. Verma. 1998. Glaciological and Geological Source of Vedic Saraswati in the Himalayas, *Itihas Darpan*, Vol. IV, No. 2: 7-36.

Radhakrishna, B.P. and S.S. Merh (eds.). 1999. *Vedic Sarasvati: Evolutionary History of a Lost River of Northwestern India*. Memoir 42. Bangalore: Geological Society of India.

Raikes, Robert. 1968. Kalibangan: Death from Natural Causes. *Antiquity*, XLII: 286-91.

Rao, S.R. 1979. *Lothal—A Harappan Port Town (1955-62)*, Vol. I. New Delhi: Archaeological Survey of India.

——. 1982. *The Decipherment of the Indus Script*. Bombay: Asia Publishing House.

——. 1985. *Lothal—A Harappan Port Town* (*1955-62*), Vol. II, New Delhi: Archaeological Survey of India.

Renfrew, C. 1988. *Archaeology and Language*. New York: Cambridge University Press.

Richter-Ushanas, E. 1992. *The Fifth Veda: The Indus Seals in Comparison with the Ṛigveda*. Germany.

Shaffer, Jim G. (in press). Migration, Philology and South Asian Archaeology. In J. Bronkhorst and M. Deshpande (eds.), *Aryan and Non-Aryan in South Asia: Evidence, Interpretation and Ideology*.

Sharma, R.S. 1999. *Advent of the Aryans in India*. New Delhi: Manohar Publishers.

Singh, Bhagwan. 1995. *The Vedic Harappans*. New Delhi: Aditya Prakashan.

Vats, M.S. 1940. *Excavations at Harappa*. 2 vols. Delhi: Government of India.

Wheeler, R.E.M. 1947. Harappa 1946: The Defences and Cemetery R 37. *Ancient India*, 3: 58-130.

Yash Pal *et al*. 1984. Remote Sensing of the 'Lost' Sarasvati River. In B.B. Lal *et al*. (eds.), *Frontiers of the Indus Civilization*, pp.491-97. New Delhi: Books and Books.

Yoganand Shastri. 1999. *Prāchīna Bhārata men Yaudheya Gaṇarājya*. New Delhi: Prāchīna Bhāratīya Itihāsa Śodha Pariṣad.

SANSKRIT TEXTS

Bhagvadgītā

Mahābhārata

Ṛigveda

Śatapatha Brāhmaṇa

Yogasūtra

INDEX

Acharya, M., 28, 31
Adh Badri, 17, 24
Agricultural field, with criss-cross pattern of ploughling, Harappan and even now, 38, 98-100
Alamgirpur, 78, 80, 96
  Late Harappans at, 78, 96
  pāṭā (for rolling bread), 78, 96
Amri, 27
Animal-sacrifice, during Harappan times, 119-120
'Aryan Invasion of India' — a myth, 67-76
Ājñā-chakra, 128
Āpayā, river, 3, 9
*Āsana*s, yogic, evidence during Harappan times, 127-128
Āvestā, 7, 9

Banawali, 39-41, 55, 59-64, 72-74, 87, 101, 121
  Early Harappa Culture, 39-41
  Mature Harappa Culture, 59, 61
    Citadel, 61-62
    'fire-altar', 63, 121
    general layout, 62
    hour-glass-shaped wristlet, 87
    Lower Town, 61-62
    moat, 62
    ploughshares, terracotta models, 101
    spoked wheels, 72, 73, 74
    touchstone bearing gold streaks, 63, 87
Banerjee, R.D., 25
Bata, terrace, 16-17
Bata-Markanda Divide, 24
Bead-making, during Harappan times at Lothal and even now, 113
Bedspreads, similarity between Harappan times and now, 114
Bhagvadgītā, 128, 132
  reference to *varṇa* system, 132
  reference to yoga, 128
Bhagwanpura, further dilution of Harappan features, 78
Biological continuity from *c* 4500 BC to *c* 800 BC, 76
Bisht, R.S., 26, 40, 41, 62, 72, 87
Bokonyi, Sandor, his identification of horse remains at Surkotada, 71
Brāhmī script, 133, 134, 135
Bullock-carts, similarity between Harappan and present ones, 107

Cage, for keeping birds, Harappan and present, 92
Caland, W., 22
Cart-tracks, similarity between Harappan times and now, 107
Cemetery H Complex, 76
Centre of Christ-consciousness, 128
Chariot, copper model comparable to modern *ekka* of Uttar Pradesh, 107
Chautang, 12, 42
Chess, 89, 91
Chitra, king, 4
Cholistan, 12, 19, 22, 26, 48
Collyrium, its use in Harappan times and even now, 88-89
Comb (*kakai*), squarish, with teeth on opposite sides, used in Harappan times and even now, 88
Cone, an ornament of gold, from Harappan levels of Mohenjo-daro, etc.; is used by Hindu women even now, 84
Cot (*chārapāi*), similarity between Early Harappan times and now, 114
Criss-cross layout of streets, Harappan, early historical and modern, 95

Dabar kot, 47
Dales, G.F., 67
Dams, on streams, Harappan (at Dholavira), 103
Dhalewan, Early Harappan Culture, 45
Dholavira, 26, 102, 103
  unique town-planning, 26
  dams on streams, 103
  well, indicating a system of drawing water with leather-bags pulled up by bullocks, 102-103
Dhyāna (meditation), probable evidence during Harappan times, 128
Dice, cubical, with 1-6 blind holes, used during Harappan times and even now, 92
Dikshit, K.N., his excavations at Hulas, 78
Dogs, collared, during Harappan times and even now, 92
Dṛiṣadvatī, 3, 12, 42

Early Harappan Culture, 26-45
Elephants, decorating elephants during Harappan times and even now, 126
'English bond', use of headers and stretchers in successive courses in walls, Harappan and modern, 94
'Extinction' of Harappan Culture—a myth, 67-77

Fairservis, W.A., 132
'Fire-altars', during Harappan times, 50, 63, 121-123
Flam, Louis, 14
Flooring, with terracotta nodules and charcoal, Harappan and modern, 94, 95
Folk tales, some going back to Harappan times, 114-116

Gamanwala, 28

Gamesmen, used in Harappan times and even now, 89, 92
Ganweriwala, 48
Gaṅgā-Yamunā Doāb, movement of Late Harappans to the upper plain of, 77
Garibnath, terrace, 16, 17
Girdle (*karadhanī*), used in Harappan times and even now, 87
Ghaggar, 11, 12, 16, 17
Goldstucker, 68
Griffith, Ralph T.H., 2, 10
Gupta, S.P., 8

Habib, Irfan, 10, 11
    his misrepresentation of the Ṛigvedic data by stating that the Sarasvati lay between the Sindhu and Sarayū, 10
Hakra
    culture, 26, 27
    river, 12, 14, 16
Harakhvati, a river in the *Āvestā*, 9
Harappa, 25, 89, 101, 107, 119, 126, 127, 130
    cart-tracks, 107
    grain-thrashing platforms, 101
    terracotta figurine, greeting with *namaste*, 126, 127
    terracotta tablet, depicting the act of sacrificing a buffalo in front of Śiva, 119
    three-in-one toiletry object in metal, 89
    workmen's quarters, 130
Harappan script, various claims, but still undeciphered, 132-134
Helmand, in Afghanistan, wrongly identified with the Ṛigvedic Sarasvatī, 8-10
Hemphill, B.E., *et al.*, their conclusion regarding biological continuity from *c* 4500 BC to 800 BC, 76
Horse, its presence in the Harappan Culture at Surkotada, Mohenjodaro and Lothal, 71
House-plan, Harappan and in present villages, 93
Hulas, Late Harappans at, 78

Iqbal, Allama, his verse on continuity of Indian culture, 136

Jalwali, 28
Jamadar, glacier, 17
Jarrige, J.-F., 83
Jha, N., 132, 133
Jhukar complex, 76
Jones, William, 7
Joshi, J.P., 26, 48, 78

Kamaṇḍalu, used in Harappan times and even now, 98
Kant, Vishnu, 45
Khatri, J.S., 28, 31
Kalibangan, 22, 26, 33-39, 44, 48-59, 73, 95, 98, 114, 118, 120, 121, 123
    design of bedspread, Early Harappan, 114
    earliest agricultural field, 26, 38, 98
    earliest earthquake, 38, 39

Early Harappan Culture, details of, 33-39, 114
general layout of site, 33
Mature Harappan Culture, 22, 48-59
animal led for sacrifice, engraving on a terracotta 'cake', 120
Citadel, 48, 50
end of settlement and radiocarbon dating, 22, 38
evidence of social stratification, 129, 130
'fire-altars', 50, 121, 123
funerary practices, 55
liṅga-cum-*yoni*, terracotta model, 118
Lower Town, layout and fortification-wall, 50-52
sacrificial pit, with animal bones, 50, 120, 123
spoked wheel, 73
*tandūr*s, 95
Kenoyer, J.M., 26, 67, 89, 108, 119
Kernos, 55
Kot Diji, 33, 47
Kotla Nihang, 26
Krishna Rao, M.V.N., 132
Kunal, 29-32, 47, 85, 87
discular necklace of silver, 31, 85
Early Harappan Culture, 28-32
spiralled bangles of silver, 31, 32, 87

Lal, B.B., 22, 26, 31, 38, 39, 47, 62, 75, 95, 130, 132, 133
Landsat imagery, 12
*Liṅga*s and *yoni*s, Harappan times and now, 118, 119
Lothal, 26, 46, 71, 87, 108, 113-115, 121
bead-making, 113
boats, 108
discular necklace of gold, 87
earliest dockyard, 26, 108
folk tales, painted on pottery, 114
horse, 71
warehouse, 46

Mackay, E.J.H., 41, 71, 134
Madhu Bala, 45, 114
Mahatma Gandhi, his philosophy of cultural openness, 137
Mahābhārata, 3
Mahiṣa-mardana (?), concept of, during Harappan times, 119
Markanda, 16
Marshall, John, 25, 41, 68, 107, 118
Masks, used in Harappan times and even now, 89
Mature Harappan Civilization, rise of, 45-67
Meadow, Richard, 46
Mehrgarh, 83
Misra, V.N., 47
Mohenjo-daro, 25, 69, 71, 76, 84, 87, 101, 107, 117, 118, 128, 134
dancing girl, bronze, wearing spiralled bangles, 87
gold cone, head-ornament, 84
limestone figure of 'priest' in *dhynāna-mudrā*, 128

liṅgas and *yonis*, 118
ploughshares, terracotta models, 101
seal, showing boat with cabin, 107
seal, showing Śiva as Paśupati, 117
skeletal remains, 69
terracotta horse, 71
writing tablets, 134
Müller, Max, 25, 68
Mughal, M.R., 22, 26, 27, 48

Nadī-stuti hymn, 1
Nahuṣa, 2, 4
Namaste, the Hindu way of greeting, during Harappan times and even now, 127
Nara, 12, 14, 16
Nath, Amarendra, 42, 44
Nausharo, female terracotta figurine showing use of vermilion (*sindūra*) in the partition-line (*māṅga*) of the hair on the head, 83
terracotta figure, showing use of collyrium, 88
Necklaces, of discular beads of silver-gold, used by Harappans at Kunal, Lothal, etc. are used even now, 85, 87

Parpola, Asko, *et al*., 132
Pañchviṁśa Brāhmaṇa, 22
Pāṭā (*chakalā*), used for rolling bread, similarity between Harappan and present ones, 96
Plakṣa Prāsravaṇa, 22
Ploughshares, similarity between Harappan and present ones, 101
Piṭṭu, a game with terracotta discs, played by Harappan children and even now, 89
Possehl, G.L., 26, 132
Puri, V.M.K., 16, 17, 24, 77
Pūru, 9

Raikes, R.L., 77
Raini, 12, 14, 16
Rakhigarhi, 42-45, 64, 66, 67, 73, 89
general layout, 43, 44
Early Harappan Culture, 42-45
Mature Harappan Culture, 64-67
cemetery, 67
fortification, 64
potter's kiln, 66
sacrificial pit and 'fire-altars', 64
spoked wheel, 73
terracotta discs used in the game of *piṭṭu*, 89
Rangpur, 26
Rann of Kachchh, 12, 14
Rao, S.R., 26, 89, 110, 132
Rehman Dheri, 46, 47
Renfrew, Colin, 70
Richter-Ushanas, E., 132
Ṛigveda, ix, 1-12, 16, 19, 22, 68, 70, 71, 75
hymns from, 1-6, 9-12, 19, 22, 68, 70, 71, 75
Dating of, on archaeological-cum-radiocarbon basis, 22, 75
Ṛigvedic Aryans, 4
did not destroy Harappan Culture, 68-70

were nomands: a wrong conception, 70, 71
Ṛigvedic polity, 71
fortifications, 71
sea-trade, 71

Sarasvatī, 1, 2, 4-6, 8-12, 14, 16-22, 75
approximate time of its drying up, 22, 75
as a river-deity, 1, 4, 5
as an Āprī deity, along with Īḷā, Mahī and Bhāratī, 1, 5
as *devitamā*, i.e. the most respected amongst deites, 4
as a goddess, along with others, 5
as *nadītamā*, i.e. the best amongst river, 4
as Vāk, 5-6
correct identification of this Ṛigvedic river, 11-12, 14, 16
flowed from mountains to the ocean, 2, 9, 16
glacier, 17
her association with *dhī* (intellect), 5
its source and perennial water-supply, 16-22
its tributaries: Ḍriṣadvatī and Āpayā, 9
its wrong identification with the Indus, 10
its wrong identification with the Helmand of Afghanistan, 8, 9
located between Yamunā and Sutlej, 2, 9, 11
reasons for its drying up, 22

Sacrifice, of animals including that of buffalo, during Harappan times and even now, 119-120
Sahni, Daya Ram, 25
Seismic Demon, 24
Shaffer, Jim G. and Diane Lichtenstein, their views on cultural continuity, 76
Sharma, R.S., 8, 72
his incorrect identification of the Ṛigvedic Sarasvatī with the Helmand of Afghanistan, 8
his wrong view that the Harappan Civilization did not have the spoked wheel, 72
Sharma, Y.D., his excavations at Alamgirpur, 78
Sindhu Nadi, recognized by Louis Flam as the former course of the Indus in Sindh, 14
Sindūra (Vermilion), its application in the partition-line of the hair (*māṅga*) by the Harappan womenfolk, as is done even now by married Hindu women, 82, 83
Śiśupālgarh, 62, 95
Śiva, in *Paśupati* aspect, during Harappan times, 117, 118
Siwalik foothills, 24
Social hierarchy, during Harappan times, 129-132
agriculturist-cum-mercantile class, 130
labour class, 130
priestly class, 129
probable emergence of Brāhmaṇas, Vaiṣyas, etc. from Harappan hierarchy, 132

Spiralled bangles, evidence from Kunal, Mohenjo-daro 'dancing girl' and present-day Rajasthani ladies, 31, 32, 87

Spoked wheel, its presence in the Harappan Culture, 72, 73, 75
  evidence from Banawali, 72, 73
  evidence from Kalibangan, 73
  evidence from Rakhigarhi, 73

Streets, orientation along cardinal direction, Harappan, Early Historical and even now, 95

Sudanwala, terrace, 16

Supin, glacier, 17

Surkotada, Harappan Culture, 26, 71
  general, 26
  presence of the horse, 71

Sutlej, 1, 2, 12

Svastika, its use during Harappan times and even now, 124

System of drawing water from wells, Harappan times and now, 102, 103

Takhtīs (*phaṭṭīs*), used for writing during Harappan and early historical times: their similarity with those used even now, 135

Tandūrs, Early Harappan and even now, 35, 43, 95

'The Cunning Fox', folk tale going back to Harappan times, 115, 116

'The Thirsty Crow', folk tale going back to Harappan times, 115

Thrashing of grains, similarity of the method used by Harappans and present-day villagers, 101, 102

Three-in-one toiletry gadget of metal, used during Harappan times and even now, 89

Touchstone, used for testing gold in Harappan times and even now, 87, 88

Trade, as a factor in the rise of Mature Harappan Civilization, 47

Transition, from Mature to Late Harappan, 78

Tree-worship, during Harappan times, 124

Utensils, *hāṇḍī, thālī, loṭā*, Harappan and modern examples comparable, 97

Vats, M.S., 25, 84, 107

Verma, B.C., 16, 17, 24, 77

Vermilion (*sindūra*), its application in the partition-line of the hair (*māṅga*) by Harappan womenfolk as is done even now by married Hindu women, 82, 83

Wahinda, 12, 14, 16

Waist-girdle (*karadhanī*), worn during Harappan times and even now, 87

Warehouse, at Lothal, 46

Water-lifting from wells, by means of large leather bags pulled up by bullocks—a system used by Harappans and even now, 102, 103

Wheeler, Mortimer, 69, 76, 107

Whitney, 68

Wilson, H.H., 68

Wristlet, of hour-glass (*ḍamaru*-like)

shape, evidence from Banawali and at present, 87
Writing tablets (*takhtīs*), similarity between Harappan examples and present ones, 134, 135

Yamunā river, 1, 2, 16, 17, 77
Yamunā Tear, 24
Yash Pal, *et al.*, 12
Yogananda Shastri, 135
Yogasūtra, of Patañjali, 127, 128, 132

Zimmer, 10